POLITICS VS. PREJUDICE IN THE HIGHWAY PATROL

Based on a true story

Reynaldo Laureano

POLITICS VS. PREJUDICE IN THE HIGHWAY PATROL

Published by Reynaldo Laureano

Printed in the United States of America

ISBN 978-0-615-30368-0

TABLE OF CONTENTS

CHAPTER ONE

Sin City - An ironic place to start

It was summer of 1984 and my father had moved the family from the tropics of Fort Lauderdale to the dry desert of Las Vegas. We did not have much to our names. Two cheap cars and a U-haul truck full to the brim with the typical items and articles families are known to drag around when moving from place to place. My father found a cheap place for us in a run-down neighborhood located just east of downtown Las Vegas. The neighborhood was rough so my brother and I spent most of the summer indoors watching the 84 Olympics which was being televised out of Los Angeles. There was no place for the neighborhood kids to hang out other than a vacant desert lot just across the back alley. The lot was mostly used by illegal dumpers and the usual sight was scattered junk and an occasional abandoned car. It was located next to an apartment complex that had a lot of foot traffic. I often suspected that it was mainly occupied by narcotic users and traffickers. There was not much for a fifteen year old to do in Las Vegas. The town was not known to be a family-oriented town. Simply put, it was a rat hole in disguise. The closest thing to friendliness was the false smiles the local casinos used to keep money-seekers coming back. A vast epidemic of anti-social disorder ruled over its counter part and infested the city like the desert smog. The town had its way with its faithful patrons and they made sure nothing got in the way. If anyone knew the secrets to getting the patrons in the door, this place wrote the book on it. Las Vegas could take a homeless mother with two infants and a purse full of baby formula out of the local bus terminal. It could put her in a cocktail waitress outfit and nab a fish without a worm on a line. Casino patrons would worship her like Cleopatra on steroids. It could take the sleaziest drug addict with a criminal record as long as the Old LA Highway off the streets of downtown and put her in a topless Vegas showroom costume and sell every seat in the house, all before sunset. Every warm body occupying a seat in front of a slot machine received a complimentary drink on the house. Alcohol for the patrons was considered money in the bank, for the house that is. And if too much alcohol took over your blood system you might even contribute to the financial gain of city hall with a little help from the local police. It worked out great for everyone in town and all were welcome to this masquerade.

But in contrast to the dim side of immoral compulsion, quietly nested in every corner of town one could find traces of the charm and rich heritage of the Latino people. Like many Border States and cosmopolitan cities, Hispanic families contributed to society like any other place shedding their Spanish traditions and pristine culture with their sometimes unwelcoming neighbors. Often chastised and sometimes viewed as an encroachment, their rich heritage and social nature was often overshadowed by a strong dislike for diversity and branded as a nuisance that even this sinful oasis could not conceal.

School kicked in and I had the privilege of being zoned to Las Vegas High School. It was a short walk from the house which took me through the dingy downtown streets past moochers and vagabonds. Every now and then I would make a routine stop at a small convenience store along the way which sat one block from the Las Vegas Strip. I vividly recall the morning a middle aged man entered the store with a peculiarly dirty foam cup in his hands. He walked over to the coffee dispenser and helped himself to a cup of coffee. He then walked past the cashier, placed two quarters on the counter, and walked out the door and around towards the back of the store. The cashier looked over at me and told me that the man was parked in the back of the store and was living out of his car. This did not come as a surprise to me until the cashier informed me that his wife and two kids were living in there with him. At that point I paused in amazement and thought to myself "Welcome to Las Vegas."

That fall I happened to stumble upon a Southern California newspaper that someone had tossed off onto a corner table in the classroom. I rarely read the paper but that day for some reason I decided to flip through the pages and came upon an interesting article. The article was about an incident that occurred one afternoon in a small suburban town on the east side of Los Angeles County. The local authorities got a call from a citizen and were asked to respond to a busy intersection where two police officers were directing traffic. What was unusual about this situation was that the lights were operating normal and there were no signs of a collision between vehicles. The officers were wearing two distinct uniforms meaning they were from different agencies and there was no patrol car in sight. So when the local police responded they discovered that the officers in question were not officers but police explorers instead. One from the Los Angeles County Sheriff's Office and the other from the local police department. Neither one was performing agency assigned duties nor did they have the legal authority to be redirecting traffic at this location. All this to say the article was quite interesting and I had learned something new. The next day I started calling around town and inquiring with the local law enforcement agencies about their explorer posts. Of the four departments I called only one returned my call. The call was that of the Nevada Highway Patrol and a representative of their explorer post had invited me to spend the next few hours with them at their weekly meeting. Little did I know this event would be the beginning of a long series of events down a road filled with obstacles of deception, bias, and greed. A challenging journey where politics and prejudice collide and where the letter of the law is put to the test to untangle an array of broken policies and a bad case of rogue politicians.

The next few months would serve as a learning experience. At just fifteen I got a first hand look at what law enforcement was all about. The over-all experience with this explorer post was exciting and gratifying. There were nights where I was asked to sit in with the dispatchers and observe what takes place on the other end of the radio. In the mid 80's there were only ten troopers assigned to the entire south end of the State of Nevada. That's a lot of ground to cover for just ten guys. I vividly recall the night a trooper working the south end of Clark County conducted a traffic stop and requested a back-up unit. His back-up was forty miles away. There were other memorable events like the time the local air force base invited all Southern Nevada explorer posts to participate in a two day military style training session. There were even times when the local big name hotel country clubs would ask the posts to provide security during tournaments. The task was simply and only required our presence in uniforms to help deter any possible wrong-doings. One July we even set up a fireworks stand to raise funds for the post. But somewhere along the way the dark side of law enforcement showed its face in a manner that I would remember for years to come. One night while attending our regular Thursday night reunion I was standing around listening and observing like any shy and some-what quiet fifteen year old would do when I overheard a conversation between the trooper assigned to lead the explorers bragging about the day he found himself on routine patrol along a lonely desert highway somewhere between Las Vegas and Reno. He came upon a vehicle parked along the side of the highway and as he approached the vehicle he noticed it was unoccupied with no driver or passengers in sight. But what he did see was a fairly new and quite expensive looking camera in one of the passenger seats. He then pulled out his baton and shattered the window grabbing the camera and admiring his new prize possession. After hearing this confession my jaw dropped to the ground as I stood their flabbergasted as to what I just heard. The shocking reality of what goes on behind the uniform hit me like the 9:00 am express train. Fairly new to the environment and loving every minute of this privileged opportunity to go behind the scenes and experience the life of a State Trooper. To think that every time

I looked at the uniform and the man behind it I would think to myself that someday that would be me. What is a fifteen year old kid to think? The years to come would only prove that this unexpected encounter was only the tip of the iceberg. There was a lot more to come.

No license to drive and a lousy public transportation system at the time forced me to leave Explorer Post 555 after nine months. Short lived but educational for the most part. Las Vegas has since gone through a lot of changes since the 80's. As the city and its surrounding area grew so did the local law enforcement agencies and the resources needed to do the job. And that's not the only thing that grew. The town's greed and arrogance grew right along with it. Add a touch of positive thinking to fuel the fire of deception and the sky was the limit.

During the summer of the following year I landed a job at one of the local casinos. It was owned by one of the largest hotels in town and managed by the typical arrogant and selfish crowd. I took a position cleaning tables in the snack bar's dining area. We had a reputation for being the only joint on the strip that sold foot long hot dogs and shrimp cocktails each for ninety nine cents. It was a hit with the crowd and still going strong till today. I had the pleasure of cleaning up after everyone's left-over garbage and after a few weeks I was assigned to the graveyard shift. Graveyard was an interesting shift. I would shuffle from table to table tending to my duties as I watched people deposit their life savings by the hundreds. They would play the slot machines for hours and jump up and down yelling like there was no tomorrow after hitting a five dollar jackpot. When the late hours of the night came around the action slowed to a crawl and standing only throwing distance from the machines I caught a glance of every bit of late night activity humanly possible. That was also about the same time management came around to empty out the five gallon buckets of cash that sat underneath every slot machine. There it went, the final resting place of sold food stamps and social security checks left behind by the wonderful patrons. It took two good size security guards and a floor supervisor to push that five hundred gallon cart of coins all the way to the vault. It never ceased to amaze me the amount of cash left behind by the crowd at the end of the day. And as the sun came up the following morning you could see the action slowly start to come alive. I sometimes shook my head in disbelief, but they came back every night right on schedule. A few hours after sunrise and the routine started all over again. I often asked myself if there was anything a guy could learn about this place. The usual answer that came to mind was that it was probably better not to know. In its own strange way it was an educational experience. And working on the strip also taught me a little about life. It would teach me a thing or two for the years to come. But the one that stuck out more then everything else was the masterful art of the sale. Arrogance, greed, and believe it or not, positive thinking would close the deal every time. These three principles resembled a perfect pyramid scheme but in a uniquely camouflaged way.

One of the most effective tools this town could count on was free advertising. As sure as the sun would rise tomorrow, for every broke loser that went back to their corner of the nation selling his trumped up tales of raining cash came a hundred more. They say sexuality sells, but this place put it on the map. Sexuality has always been a guaranteed seller. It's been a marketing tool since the beginning of time. Very much like the candy behind the glass. Like a faithful friend standing by your side, sexuality and this town went hand-in-hand all the way to the bank.

One afternoon while on my way to the employee dining room I entered an elevator with a guy headed towards the casino that just couldn't stay still. He acted like he was ready to run a marathon. He pointed at the elevator button displaying the letter "C" for casino and then looked over at me and said "C stands for cash." I watched as the guy got off the elevator and walked off dancing in the hallway as I said to myself, "C also stands for chapter 7 bankruptcy."

In early 1989 I ventured off to the National Guard hoping to launch a career as a pilot only to be told that the Guard was not looking for pilots at the time. After reviewing a list of potential careers I chose that of a Military Policeman. Not long after enlisting I was released for Active Duty and spent the next few years with the US Army where I was eventually assigned to Frankfurt, Germany. Those next few years were a learning experience. I met some very dedicated soldiers and some not so dedicated. Early from basic training we were warned about the pros and cons of law enforcement. I recall a Sergeant asking us to look around the room. He warned us that many of the faces around us would eventually be dismissed or simply washed away in the revolving door of law enforcement. And he was right.

The next few years we saw everything within the ranks. We saw everything from theft to drug use, by all ranks, ages, and races. There were rackets, scandals, and plain abandonment. Not much different from our civilian counter part.

Just before shipping off to Germany I spent a week at Ft. Dix in New Jersey dealing with all the paperwork involved in military enlistment. One particular form I will never forget was the Combined Federal Campaign with its lengthy list of non-profit organizations. It has been around for years. There were some well-known names on the list such as the American Red Cross and Salvation Army. But one particular non-profit organization, so they claimed to be, got my attention and I elected to give a modest amount from my monthly pay. This so-called non-profit organization was known as the Puerto Rican Legal Defense and Education Fund also known as PRLDEF. And years later I would come to find out just how useful this legal defense organization would be. The Army did not pay a new soldier much in those days. You were lucky to receive $1000 a month if that. However, I figured a small donation would not hurt. He who gives shall receive. And that I did for the next three years. I was giving good money, to a good organization, for a good cause. So I thought. Nevertheless, I authorized the deduction from my check. Ten dollars a month was a small but noble amount.

And after a long and cold week at Fort Dix I was on my way to Europe. I made the best out of the few years in Frankfurt. I did what I did best. Got out and mingled with the locals, traveled a bit hitting the attraction parks and places of interest, and most important went full-force in pursing my pilot's certificate. The common public referred to it as a pilot's license. I found out that some of the local military installations had flying clubs and after a little investigating I was on my way scouting out the nearest one. Located in a small town about twenty miles south of the metropolitan city of Frankfurt was the military community of Darmstadt along with the Darmstadt Army Airfield. Located on the airfield was the Darmstadt Flying Club which I quickly became a regular customer of. Getting there was not easy. First, I had to hop a local subway train to the Main train station in downtown Frankfurt. And then I had to take another train to the town of Darmstadt. Walk half a mile south to an awaiting street car that would drop me off one mile north of the airfield. From this point I had to walk through a small neighborhood to the north side of the airfield where I had to show my military ID, continue across a ramp full of Blackhawk medical Evac helicopters, stop along side an active runway, look both ways for landing and departing traffic, and when the coast was clear walk across the runway to the south end of the field where the flying club was located. And when the day was done I would grab my flight bag and do the entire route all over again. Look both ways, walk across the runway, etc. Nevertheless, once I was there the fun began. For weeks to come I flew around Southern Germany enjoying the bird's eye view of the spectacular countryside. But, the military wasn't so helpful in giving its soldiers enough of an advanced notice of their off days so making plans on your days off was close to impossible and this caused a strain and in the long run a delay in me obtaining my pilot's certificate.

After three years of dedicated service it was time to come back home and see what the civilian life had to offer. I returned to Las Vegas which had not changed much in the last three years. A new hotel and casino here and a sleazy strip joint there. People still came from all over the country to make Las Vegas their new home. I never could figure out just what exactly made people want to choose Las Vegas. But they did and they came from all over averaging 4,000 new comers a months. It was soon becoming the fastest growing city in America. Back in town and at age 21 there was not much to choose from in the form of employment. I headed to the Nevada Department of Employment Security office where the receptionist directed me to the veteran representative's office. I was greeted by three older men all Veterans of the military who quickly pulled out a small stack of papers and instructed me to look them over. Not quite the red carpet treatment but what else could I expect. I was in Sin City. I went down the list looking for aviation or law enforcement related jobs but had no luck finding any. I was amazed as to what the state employment office had to offer its returning military veterans. The list consisted of mostly fast-food restaurants with close to minimum wage salaries. I remember asking the Veteran's representative where the list of aviation or law enforcement related jobs were. His response was quick and clear. What you saw was what you got. I realized that if I wanted to pursue a career in aviation or law enforcement I would have to hit the pavement and look elsewhere. In the mean time I looked at my options and the only job on the list that caught my attention was that of a radio dispatcher with an overnight delivery company called Airborne Express. So I took it and the office manager set me up with an interview that same week. My first job interview out of the military and I was off to a bad start. I had a hard time locating the place and showed up ten minutes late for the interview. As I walked in the main door I asked the receptionist for the manager and around the corner appeared a very attractive Spanish lady with a very unpleasant look on her face and she said to me "You're late!" She directed me to her office where she proceeded to conduct the interview. I mentioned the use of radios in the military and how we took turns working as dispatchers at the station and after about thirty minutes I was out the door and on my way back home. The following day I was given a job offer which I gladly accepted and found myself on the payroll that week. Months went by and during a casual conversation with the receptionist she enlightened me with some interesting information about the manager that had hired me. I was informed that my late arrival caused the manager to decide that I was not the candidate for the job but that her choices were between a late interviewee and an older guy in his mid 50's. And she was not about to hire the old guy so I was the lesser of the evils. I felt fortunate to have a job but I was not quite sure how to feel for this stranger who was clearly a victim of age discrimination. The recent years in the Army and its experiences taught me to be receptive of such comments and although I was not quite flabbergasted by this statement, it was a reassurance of the injustices one could expect in today's employment environment.

I was there for a year and a half and most of the money I earned I spent down at the local flight school located at the North Las Vegas airport. I found myself at the airfield almost two days a week and before you knew it I had achieved getting my long anticipated Private Pilot's certificate. Years of waiting had finally paid off and shortly after that I decided it was time for a well deserved vacation. There were many options to choose from and many places on my list of places to see. At the age of twenty one I had been and seen more places than many see in an entire life time courtesy of the US military. After experiencing the freedom of traveling to vast and far away places, taking away that freedom was not easy. It was a hard habit to break especially for an aviation enthusiast. But for some it was not hard at all. Many of our fellow soldiers returned to their respective homes of enlistment scattered throughout the country. Many of us kept in touch throughout the years to come but very few had the luxury or the financial means of visiting each other. As for me, I was destined to keep the good times going.

I took a week off from work and elected to visit some former Army comrades who were living in the State of Tennessee. The short visit to this area consisted of some sight-seeing in and around the Nashville area which included some historic towns, well-known attractions, and the very elegant and luxurious Opryland Hotel situated just off the banks of the Cumberland River. After experiencing the southern aspect of this picturesque region of the country, I was able to check off one more spot on my map of places explored. With its varied terrain, enchanted rivers, and enormous lakes, it made for a setting quite different from the arid desert of the great southwest and the abundance in vegetation was an overwhelming sight for sore eyes which hadn't seen so much green in previous years. After concluding what turned out to be a first class tour of this intriguing region courtesy of the finest products of the US Army, I was so impressed with the visit that I told all to my friends and just about everyone I knew that if I ever decided to move out of Las Vegas I would strongly consider the Nashville area. With its affordable living expenses, relatively low crime, and now hiring signs at virtually every corner, it seemed like a place certainly worth looking into. Not too far down the road, that's exactly what I did.

CHAPTER TWO

The road to good intentions

Three months later and years of nothing but dry sun and desert made me decide it was time for a change. I called the guys in Tennessee and told them I was on my way. I packed everything I owned in the back seat of a 1990 Chevy Camero sports coupe and headed east. The two day journey was spectacular and had a lot to see. Across Hoover Dam and Lake Mead and down towards Kingman in Arizona where I took Interstate 40 east along old Route 66 headed towards the painted desert. Across lakes and mountains, the mighty Mississippi River, and finally rolling hills and lots of green grass. Forty eight hours later and 1945 miles I pulled up to a small town called Clarksville in the northern part of Tennessee. Sleepy and exhausted I came upon the town square at about midnight. I made one wrong turn and I found myself lost in downtown Clarksville. My atlas only showed major roads in and around the small town but nothing with the city streets. Lost and dozing off behind the wheel I made a prayer and it was answered. I came around a corner and in the middle of nowhere like an oasis in the desert was a Holiday Inn motel. There it was in the middle of downtown Clarksville with only one vacant parking spot left with my name written all over it. I pulled up, checked in, and called it a night.

The next day I met up with my old Army buddy Dennis who lived in a small but quiet trailer park in a tiny town along the interstate. He and his wife happened to mention that the trailer next to them was unoccupied and after a trip to the leasing office I walked out with a key to the trailer. A bit run down but it was better then nothing. The next day I found myself once again at the unemployment office but this time with the State of Tennessee. The receptionist directed me to the veteran's representative who was kind and helpful. He handed me a list of jobs to look over and to my surprise the options consisted of approximately three pages of, you guessed it, mostly fast-food restaurants with close to minimum wage salaries. Talk about DéjàVu. I asked the veteran representative if there were any aviation or law enforcement related positions that he was aware of. His answer was "No." For a town located outside a major US Army installation it was clear that this office had very little to offer its veterans. I did notice a dispatcher position with the security guard company that worked at the town's community college. I thought it over and decided to skip this time around. I then thought to myself "Hit the pavement." With not many options in that small town I got up early the next day and headed down to the metropolitan city of Nashville where I met up with another Army friend and quickly took to the streets looking for work. The first stop was the Nashville International Airport where I knocked on doors and inquired about jobs. There was not much to choose from there but I was fortunate to land a part time gig as a security guard at the C & D concourse security checkpoint at the airport terminal. It paid minimum wage and only lasted four months. I headed down to the local Airborne Express office only to be told that they were not hiring at the time. As I headed back to the interstate that would take me in the direction of Clarksville I noticed a large hanger adjacent to the airport runway. And along side the hanger were a pair of Bell Jetranger helicopters with the words Tennessee State Trooper displayed along both sides of the aircraft. It donned on me that I was looking at the Tennessee Highway Patrol's aviation division. Just off to the east side of the hanger was the area headquarters of the Tennessee Highway Patrol. I went inside and asked about their recruiting process and what it would take to get in with the aviation unit. I was referred to the state personnel office where the whole recruiting process begins. Another stop was added to the list but for the following day. The last stop of the day was the majestic Opryland Hotel. I had such a memorable time during my vacation visit that is seemed like a pleasant place to work. A trip to their employment office resulted in me landing a job as a front desk agent. Four months later I took on the position of valet parker and eventually that of a Bellman where I remained until my last days there. The hotel would be an exciting place to work but it would only be temporary. Three year's experience in law enforcement, veteran status, a crystal clear record, and a few thousand dollars invested in a pilot's certificate should open doors in this intriguing region of the country which was well-known for its southern hospitality and old fashion charm. But even Nashville had its own devious and distinctive ways. And its well-kept secrets leaked like the dams and locks along the Tennessee River. Turning a new leaf was not as easy as I thought it would be. It came with its challenges. I would soon find that deep beneath the tranquil southern setting and not too different from its desert counterpart, unrevealing Nashville's well-kept secrets would not be taken too kindly and it came with a price. Not to mention a not-so-secret habit that this fertile metropolis dreaded on its every reminder. An age long habit that was very hard to break. Out with the old and in with the new at age twenty one did not mean much. It was just a popular saying. What I saw in Sin City I thought would be unmatched anywhere else. Las Vegas may have been the king of the hill in its own category but I would soon discover that Music City would give Sin City a run for its money in a different kind of way. It was then that I had realized that maybe Las Vegas was not all that bad after all.

CHAPTER THREE

Let the games begin

In July of 1993 I took a drive downtown and appeared at the state testing center where I was given a written test and was fortunate to score in the 80's. Two months later I was invited to my first interview at the Nashville area highway patrol station just down the road from the Nashville International Airport. Dressed in a three piece suit, a leather briefcase, and a military style high-and-tight hair cut I presented myself like a salesman ready to land a million-dollar contract. Pointing out many positive traits about myself, I laid on some of the most important issues such as my ability to speak the Spanish language and the importance of agency's need to communicate with a fast growing immigrant community who commonly lacked the ability to speak the English language. I included several other useful issues but the most important of them all, my interest in eventually moving up to the elite aviation division. I focused on topics such as the money the agency would save in having an already trained and licensed pilot. Little did I know that sales pitch was falling on deaf ears. Three weeks after the interview I received my first rejection letter from the state. This letter would be one I would become very familiar with in the years to come and as the years went by I remained on the eligibility roster and was invited to several interviews in the years to follow. Every interview was for the same position and all ended with the same results.

In December of 1993 the lucky contestants prepared for the academy and it was also about that time that I met a Hispanic man known to be very active in the Hispanic community. Mario Ramos was a lawyer, probably the only Hispanic lawyer in the city of Nashville at the time, who was very dedicated to the advancement and well-being of the fast growing Hispanic community. After a brief meeting and an exchange of interests we discovered that we had a lot in common. Mario was also well informed and current on the interests of local politicians and community leaders and he often updated me on the various government jobs which often resulted from their claims of seeking out Hispanic applicants. I would later discover that many were just that, allegations by area politicians and various government agency administrative personnel feeding the people of the community public relations lines with no statistical backing to support their claims.

But Mario was an impressive individual who turned out to be very dedicated to this cause. Event after event he helped organize Latino community events such as the annual Cinco de Mayo festivals. If it dealt with the Hispanic community he was there or he knew about it. And he did an excellent job of keeping me informed as well. As the months went by I found myself mingling with the crowd and although I was nothing close to an entrepreneur my face no longer got lost in the crowd. As the years went by I became more and more involved. Whether it was to keep from being bored or just looking for the opportunity to meet people in high places, I made it a point to be there.

In 1994 I stumbled upon a different line of work. One afternoon I was sitting at home watching TV when a commercial came on TV that caught my attention. A regional trucking company was looking to recruit drivers and money was a lot better than what I was making parking cars at the hotel so I called the number on the screen and they set me up with an appointment with their local recruiter. One month later I was attending a local truck-driving school and after three weeks I was holding a class "A" commercial driver's license. The following month I was behind the wheel and on the road. The job paid well but demanded a lot. The crowd was unique. I saw a little bit of everything and met people from all corners of the country and all walks of life. The trucking crowd lacked a little bit of social skills but not much to be concerned about. In this line of work I got to meet and worked with people from all different walks of life and a few with dark and fairly odd backgrounds.

I started driving with a regional carrier which required at least three weeks with a driver trainer. The company paired me up with what started off as a jolly-go-lucky character but later turned into a Dr. Jeckle and Mr. Hyde. This actor lived in a small town along the Tennessee River about ninety miles west of Nashville which was not all that far from my place. And that was about all we had in common. I was off to a good start in my training days until the point where he claimed to have been a professional thief and later serving five years in the pen. Not what I wanted to hear. I kept my past experience as a military policeman to myself and only talked about aviation. As the days went by I discovered that this fellow was in desperate need of an income and kept the wheels rolling with very few breaks in between. The breaks were brief and limited to fuel stops, pick-ups, and deliveries. The only music he ever listened to was Christian music which I later realized was part of his act to make himself look like a bible seeking born again Christian. I almost started to suggest that if he had fifteen minutes for a hot dog break he could just as easily spend half that time at the truck stop shower. But not knowing just how true his story about being an ex-convict was I figured it was best to keep that suggestion to myself.

For the next five days we covered everything from Texas to Illinois, listening to fake stories and not a shower in sight. And there I was cooped up with a wolf in sheep's clothing listening to what appeared to be fabricated stories which seemed to get worse as the days went by. When the weekend arrived he offered to drop me off at the house that Friday evening with the understanding that we would meet up Sunday night and proceed on to the next pick up point. We stopped at his house so I could become familiar with the location and after a short tour of his pathetic, caveman-style house we were off to mine. Whatever his income building tactics were it was clear that they were not working. His house had holes in the floor so big you could put your fist through it. The walls were no different and the entire place was quite nasty with an unpleasant odor floating in the air. The place was truly a rat hole. What I found rather strange was the fact that he had no form of dependable communication, such as a telephone, and that he depended on a fellow church member who lived across town to deliver his phone messages. A telephone at home is a very important tool for anyone who works in the transportation industry. For a family man and a father of three still living at home, this actor demonstrated more of a trashy lifestyle by the minute. As the years went by I would later discover that this type of lifestyle went hand-in-hand with the trucking industry and year by year I reminded myself that the primary reason for enduring and tolerating this sub-standard environment was to build wealth for a better tomorrow.

I enjoyed the short lived two days off and on Sunday hitched a ride by air from a friend who owned a small plane based out of the Lebanon airport to the small airport of Camden just across the Tennessee River. After a short forty five minute flight in pure cloud cover we landed in this small town airport and attracted some attention from the few by-standers that were hanging out at the airport. The fuel attendant came out and filled the tanks and told use how rare it was for a couple of young pilots to just pop in like we did. He told us that most of the pilots that stopped in and hung out at this airfield were mostly older guys. A pilot without gray hair was an odd sight at this place. After topping the tanks and paying the bill he was off and on his return trip to the Lebanon Airport. We touched down just before sunset and after a short conversation with the fuel attendant he informed me that the only cab service in this small town did not run on Sundays. However, he offered to give me a lift to a laundromat two miles down the road not far from his place of residence. Two hours later I marched up the main drag towards the town square and then west a few blocks until I arrived at his house. After ringing the door bell this self

proclaimed ex-convict informed me, in a rather rude and hateful manner, that the departure time had been changed to the following morning and lodging for that night was at the truck which was located sixteen miles south at the truck stop. I asked him to explain to me what had happened and why the changes in the itinerary. It appeared that this scoundrel had called the company and requested an earlier pick up time which the company managed to work out with the customer. And after attempting to contact me to inform me of the changes he became disgruntled when told that I was not available to take the call. Maybe that was because I was at 3,000 feet above the earth and somewhere over Middle Tennessee with no access to a pay phone. He later scrambled to undo the mess he created and held a grudge against me for the rest of the day. I tried to explain my circumstances but it was of little concern to him as he repeatedly informed me that my bed for that night was in the truck sixteen miles south. I asked him if he would be so kind as to drive me to the truck stop or even the motel down the street only to have the door slammed in my face. I said to myself "I guess that means no." So I turned towards the poorly unlit street and started walking back towards the town square. The sun had just gone down and there was silence up and down the street except for the dogs barking at me as I marched in the darkness block by block. I kept asking myself if I could make the trip by foot since it was such a long distance. It had been six years since I had walked such a distance and that was when I was in basic training in the Army. Ten and fifteen mile hikes were common in those days but there was a bad side to all of this. The highway was a dark and lonely highway which stretched through the south end of the county leading towards Interstate 40 which is where the truck was located. Hitch-hikers were known to be mugged, robbed, and there have even been cases of those left for dead. Walking alongside a dark and lonely highway after midnight was one thing I really did not care to do. Besides, it would take me every bit of eight hours to make the trip. When I got to the square I saw a police car and came up with the courageous idea of asking the local cops for a helping hand. I explained my situation and they referred me to the sheriff's office two blocks south which had jurisdiction of that area of the county. I headed two blocks down and walked up to the desk and spoke to the dispatcher working that evening who told a pair of deputies of my dilemma. They seemed like descent folks and were kind enough to give me a ride down to the truck stop. I remember overhearing one of the deputies telling the dispatcher to avoid making any radio transmissions about the ride and it was clear to me that there was a policy against using police vehicles as a taxi cab service. I was embarrassed and somewhat nervous. These deputies did not know who I was or whether my story was true of false. The first few minutes of the ride gave me an uneasy feeling. The silence in the patrol car made me think the worst. I did not know just what was going through their minds and they did not know what was going through mine. But one of the deputies broke the ice and began asking me about truck driving and what I thought about it. There really wasn't much to tell except that I was looking for a better income and although not my number one career choice it would make do for now. I expressed how I felt about the dirty side of the trucking industry. They asked me if my trainer and I had had a disagreement and I told them the whole story. I explained to them that I was a new driver and the misunderstanding that had occurred with my driver-trainer and it was almost like they had heard the story all too many times before. It made perfect sense after realizing that any call, complaint, or interaction with any suspicious person that came in from the truck and diesel stops fell in their assigned area and cases like mine were a dime a dozen. The little bit of conversation I had with them was good and I was very grateful for their assistance and for once in a very long time I got a chance to see the side of police work that makes an officer go beyond his normal scope of duties in providing service to his community. Something you don't see a lot of these days.

The patrol car pulled up to the dining room side of the truck stop and I got out of the back seat. All eyes were on me. I looked like a prisoner being escorted into jail. I thanked them and headed towards the truck embarrassed and feeling like a rodent. As I approached the cab of the truck I felt like a peasant returning to a make-shift dog house. I thought to myself "Is this the price that I have to pay to earn a few more dollars?" Even more "Does one have to stoop down so low as to beg for an opportunity to get ahead in life?"

As I walked through the dark and dreary parking lot I could smell the urine that lingered throughout the pavement from drivers who chose to relieve themselves just outside the driver's door to save them the inconvenience of walking a few more feet to the restrooms inside. It was a common smell that I got used to coming in and out of the parking areas mostly after sundown. I found myself tired and sleepy yet trying to fight the state of disgust which seemed to be getting worse as the exhaust from the idling diesel engines and the heat blowing out from the grills hit me in the face as I walked between the trucks lined up in perfect order. I looked over my shoulder and around the corners of the giant hoods and grills ready for unexpected crooks and thieves who often targeted truck stops and drivers as easy prey. As I approached the cab-over International that was assigned to us, I thought about the many years that I had spent and wasted government resources and tax dollars dealing with dirtbags like these. Experiences both good and bad, and the few times I had the privilege of checking them into the cross-bar hotel. I tried to convince myself to ignore it all, not to let it bother me, and that there was always a price to pay to get ahead. I pulled out my set of keys, opened the passenger's side door, and climbed up into the cab. But something came over me and for just a moment I rationalized the whole chain of events.

In the aviation world earning your wings means dedicating time, sweat, and a considerable amount of money. You overlook the possibility of death to feel the sensation of sailing through the atmosphere. And you trade the dirty looks for what seems to be a desk job with the world's greatest view. And let's say that after all that you still haven't convinced yourself how illogical you have become, you get a small plastic card welcoming you to the privileged world of aviators. But nowhere along the way does it say that you had to bow down to scum.

I took the keys and threw them on the dash, the training book and tossed it on the driver's chair, and got down from the cab and shut the door behind me. And as I walked off I thought to myself "I don't think so. Not this kid." Years of training and the few times I had to throw someone behind bars, an impeccable record, and an honorable discharge was just enough to make me walk away with dignity.

I looked around to see what my options were. Two truck stops, a waffle house, and across the street was a motel with a neon sign flashing vacancy. As I walked towards the interstate I noticed a Greyhound bus stop sign near the front entrance of the truck stop indicating a designated drop off and pick-up point for the Greyhound Bus Company. I walked across the interstate and with the last few dollars I had paid for a room for the night. I grabbed a pay phone and called the company to firmly inform them that if they wanted me as a driver they would have to pay my way back to the terminal and set me up with a different driver. Preferably one with a little more class. As for the motel bill, this one was on me. The next morning I walked back across the interstate to the truck stop to await the next eastbound bus scheduled to make its stop in town. As I waited I could not help but notice a young African American man on the pay phone a short distance from where I was standing and who appeared to be in distress. My proximity to him caused me to unintentionally eavesdrop on his conversation which appeared to be with his dispatcher in another state. I also observed a small group of three Caucasian fuel desk employees, a female and two males. I observed as they watched over the man in distress but with a rather unpleasant facial expression. A look I was much too familiar with. An evil look of hate and disgust and as the driver explained his dilemma it was clear to me that he was having mechanical problems. A flat tire to be precise. My eyes shifted back and forth between the driver and staff like a fan in the bleachers of a tennis tournament, neither of which ever caught on to my presence. As the driver attempted to inform his dispatcher of his situation, he seemed to be unsure of his exact location and waived over to the staff as if he was asking for them to talk to his dispatcher. At first they ignored him and looked the other way as the driver continued to struggle and after his second request for help I observed as one of the male attendants, who minutes earlier was friendly and helpful to each and every customer who entered the door, shake his head sideways as to say no and walk away. I felt anger but not that much towards the employees. More for the man in distress as his naïve state blinded him from noticing his surroundings. Something made me react as I began walking towards him contemplating how discreet I could be and the proper words to use. "Listen friend, these folks have no intentions of helping you," was the only line that came to mind and I thought to myself that his best bet was for me to talk to his dispatcher and give his location. But as I got within four feet of him to offer my services he hung up the phone and not knowing my intentions walked past me and out the door towards his truck. A three minute event that stayed imprinted in my memory for the rest of my life. An opportunity to make a difference, the ability to make a change and I made the effort with good intent.

Moments later my bus pulled up and I was on my way to the Southern Indiana terminal just across the river from Louisville. The trip lasted six hours and I spent most of the trip thinking about the last few series of events that had occurred. I spent most of the trip thinking about the deputies from Benton County and although it was a very generous gesture, they did not have to do what they did. Instead of saying no they risked their jobs which paid close to minimum wage to do a kind deed of giving a stranded guy a ride. They worked an area that dealt with a lot of activity most of which was heavy interstate transient traffic. Not to mention backup as close as sixteen miles up the road. From the looks of the old Chevy Impala the county did not have enough in their budget to provide them with modern equipment but yet they came to work and made due with what the had to pay the bills. And for a part of the county that had a reputation of years of prejudice and racism they did not hesitate to give a Puerto Rican guy a ride. You don't see many police officers with that type of character. As the old saying goes "you reap what you sew" and the years to come will prove that to be true. I was back behind the wheel the next day and with a different trainer.

A week later I was on my own cruising the highways and byways of America. Six months of regional driving flew by like clock work. I covered a lot, from New York to Texas, Chicago to Florida. But even the road had its dark side. The industry's need for drivers caused a lax in the standards most companies used in their selection of drivers and as a result most truck stops and loading docks were not much of a safe haven. Long days and lonely nights behind the wheel concluded with lousy and expensive truck stop food. Every late night coffee break came with a swat team style approach as I cautiously returned to my vehicle, peeking around corners for any unexpected loiterers or would-be robbers awaiting my return. Uncooperative receiving dock personnel who chose to be hateful or simply unwilling to give helpful directions to their location would have me lost at half past midnight in the roughest neighborhoods in America. The constant vulgar language, sarcastic remarks, and racial slurs circulating on the CB radio would make the Manson family look like the Brady Bunch. The time had come to seek better options. During that year I was invited to interview for the second time by the highway patrol. There was nothing different about this interview just the faces. They asked the same questions, I answered the same lines, and I got the same results. I remained on the roster for years to come and so did the claims from both the state and the various Nashville area law enforcement agencies and their desperate search for Spanish-speaking officers.

But every now and then I would get the same question. Friends, co-workers, or just a simple acquaintance the question always came up. Why would anyone with a pilot's license be wasting their time looking for a cop job? The pay is lousy, job is dangerous, and half the guys you work with are just as bad as the guys you put behind bars. I sometimes asked myself the same question and to avoid going into a long and boring story most people would not understand anyways I would explain "There is only one route to take if you wanted to make your way into the highway patrol's elite Aviation Unit. There were no other avenues." So time and patience accompanied me down this long and lonely road to nowhere. I was left with no option but to stay where I was, so I did.

The money was good for a rookie driver but living on the road took its toll and one early Friday morning I found myself making a delivery in the city that I called home. In the center of downtown Nashville I waited in line behind a local driver who drove for another company. Our conversation eventually shifted to working with companies that gave you both the chance to drive and see home at the same time. As we compared notes I discovered that chance was just a phone call away. I made a few calls in town and drove the streets of the industrial parks and was fortunate to come upon the company that would give me just that chance. I took a job with a regional less-than-truckload outfit, also known as LTL. This company would pay me a bit more and kept me on a steady route along with a steady schedule. I ran the Atlanta route every night at 9:00 PM which brought me back home the following morning at 6:00 AM. Five days a week with weekends off. I could not ask for anything better. For years to come I pulled the loads and ran the miles. I memorized every on ramp, coffee stop, and tree stump along the way.

During March of this year I took a trip up to Hopkinsville to visit Dennis. On my way to his house I stopped at the local airport to see what it had to offer. The terminal had a charming look to it and the staff was friendly and helpful like most. I stepped into the pilot's lounge to find a flyer announcing a small airplane for sale. A 1979 Piper Tomahawk with an asking price of $15,000. I did not think much of it and never really saw myself as an aircraft owner so I left and headed towards town to spend the rest of the day at the local country club with Dennis. Two weeks later I was up to the same routine with another trip to the same airport and in the pilot's lounge the same announcement only that the asking price had dropped to $12,500. I didn't think twice and by the end of the week I was making plans to test fly what was to be my new toy. The funds exchanged hands and papers were signed. It was the start of a new beginning and like a kid walking out of a candy store with a full basket I could not wait to fly the wheels off of it. In a matter of days I was up and going.

Work at the company continued hard and heavy and the driving job lasted three and a half years. I was driving all night, flying in the mornings, and resting all day. I lived in a travel trailer which a friend once described as a shoe box. It measured six feet by ten feet with just enough room for a twin size bed which was all I needed at the time. The money was coming in and little was going out in the form of expenses. Life was good and the company was great until the day that management caught on to the fact that drivers had the word "Union" on their minds and a month later the doors were closed and we were out on the streets.

This was also the year that flying picked up. I was logging hours like crazy. Two to three times a week you would find me down at the airfield either taking a few laps around the traffic pattern or making a quick hop to a near by airport. An hour up the road was the average flying time.

In December of 1997, while hanging around the airfield I met a Puerto Rican guardsman by the name of Juan Amaro. Born on the island in a small town not far from the one I lived in as a child. Juan was a helicopter mechanic who recently left the active Army and came to the area after receiving a job offer with a large aviation maintenance company that operated a maintenance hanger out of the Nashville International Airport. That job was short lived and with luck on his side and the right timing he found himself working a full-time gig with the National Guard and assigned to the state-of-the-art Blackhawk helicopters based at the airfield. Being the social butterfly that I was I approached him and identified myself as one of the local pilots and offered to take him up for a spin on the next planned flight. As any aviation enthusiast, he jumped on the opportunity and within a week we were joy-riding at five thousand feet on our way to a not-too-distant airport in Northern Georgia for lunch. It did not take him long to realize what he had on his hands. We both knew that it wasn't everyday that a Hispanic guy would get a chance to hop a flight at no cost and go virtually anywhere in the Midwest on a weekly basis. Hispanics, like African Americans and other minority groups, were and still are a rare sight around most airfields in America. I felt as if I had contributed to opening the path that few get to travel during their lifetime. And the ventures went on for months. Atlanta, Chicago, and Philadelphia. We were jetting around the country like the rich and famous.

One spring day, while making a stop at a small airport located just north of Atlanta, I approached the fuel desk to order a quart of oil and inquire about the parking fees. The young man behind the counter was very polite and helpful. I glanced over at his co-worker who was sitting to his side reading the local paper. He was a Caucasian man in his early thirties quietly sitting to the right of his helpful co-worker. He sat there silently staring me down like a Bulldog about to charge at a rabbit. The local paper had a front page story of a plane crash that occurred a few miles north of there. I asked him if I could buy the paper from him once he was done. He answered "No!" It was worth a shot. As we exited the terminal Juan looked at me and asked "Did you see the way that guy was looking at you? It's like you were dressed in woman's clothing." I guess I was not the only one to catch on to his facial expression. It stuck out like a neon sign. I looked over at Juan and said "I am used to it," and went on to say "you will have to get used to it if you are going to be involved in aviation." He then looked around and realized we were the only minorities on the entire airfield. So we used the courtesy car to go into town and visit a friend and after having breakfast at a local restaurant we headed back to the airfield for a ninety minute flight back home. The weather was perfect, visibility went on as far as the eye could see, and the temperature was just right. It was another fine day in the world of aviation and another satisfied guest.

As the years have passed I have had the privilege of witnessing the magic and the beauty of flight and how it touches people. I have felt the rewarding pleasure of seeing its awesome ability of intriguing the imagination, its exonerating feeling of freedom, and its captivating force of gaining other's confidence and respect through an unforgettable flying experience. There is rarely an unsatisfied guest and every passenger walks away craving for more. An empty seat is a wasted seat that is going with me, empty or not. I see it as another wasted shot at making a change. Those who know me can tell you I always turn down offers of compensation. Money means nothing to me and there is no charge for this ticket to ride. My favorite saying is" The finest things are free, everything else costs money."

After a few months of no work and lots of play I landed another driving job with the second largest LTL carrier in the nation. Around October of 1999 the company laid off and I was forced to operate off of my reserve funds which quickly bottomed out. It came at me out of nowhere and I found myself in a downward spiral, and picking up speed by the second. I eventually returned to the road but from a different angle. For the first time ever I was an entrepreneur. I bought a brand new 2001 Chevrolet cargo van and returned to the industry as an expediter but I soon found out that sub-contracting was not a wise move.

During the next few years things took a turn for the worst. Expenses were up and income was down. The airplane was soon grounded only to collect spider webs and bird nests. There it remained for eight long years. 9-11 soon appeared in the picture and in addition to the enormous after-effects of this horrific event, it resulted in both commercial and general aviation taking a hit. Two months before this event I celebrated my accomplishment of obtaining my commercial pilot's license and had started sending out resumes but it was eleven years too late. Those responsible for this tragic event would cost hundreds of pilot's their jobs and would push pilot hopefuls out of the picture. The commercial side of aviation shortly recovered but general aviation suffered for years to come.

There was a period of silence, of inactivity between 1994 and 2002. It was as if I had disappeared off the files of the highway patrol and the last few years to come had put me through some ups and downs. One summer day in 2002 I was surprised to get a call from the trooper assigned the task of scheduling interviews. I was at a truck stop in Michigan where I spent most of that year delivering automotive parts to what was known as the big-four auto manufacturers. It had been so long that I thought I had fallen off the roster. So I talked with the trooper for a few moments and he informed me that he was in the process of setting up interviews. This time it was for the position of Commercial Vehicle Enforcement Officer. How ironic. I had been driving for the trucking industry for eight years now and became very familiar with the Federal Motor Carrier Safety Regulations. Not only did I have the law enforcement background, the aviation training and experience, but now I had spent the last eight years dealing with the same laws and regulations I would be enforcing. That is if I was hired for the job. Besides, it was a way in and it would only be temporary. The aviation unit would always be there and I reminded myself that there was no other way to get there but by moving up within the ranks. So I agreed to an interview and when I returned home down south I took a day off from work to make my third appearance. I rehearsed the lines that would probably be thrown at me. Prepared the same old suit, which I was surprised still fitted me, and grabbed the briefcase which was empty most of the time but it was only for looks. And don't forget to mention that commercial pilot's license, it saves the agency valuable tax dollars in training. Making an impression was what it was all about. So I thought.

Later that month I spent most of the time on the road. Most of that time was spent between Nashville and Detroit. I stayed on the road as much as I could but business was beginning to slow down some and competition was tight. It was sometime around July of 2003 that I got out of expedited trucking all together. I then took up a driving job for a friend in Nashville who had a few trucks that he needed to keep moving. The political thugs at the administrative level of the highway patrol had kicked me to the curb where I remained for the few years that followed and flying was out due to a serious lack of funds. But money began to take a turn for the better and one day while visiting Dennis across the state line in Kentucky I noticed a book sitting on his dresser written by a Nashville area radio talk show host who encouraged his readers and listeners to live a debt free lifestyle. I opened it up, read a few pages, and within no time I was hooked on his ideas. I bought his book, which was a sure road to financial success, and followed every piece of advice he had to give. Dave had been on the air for several years spreading his words of wisdom and I tuned in on the radio to every show I could catch. Not only was the money coming in it was staying in just like his book suggested. Working seven days a week and about fourteen hours a day, I was finally resurfacing like a submarine looking for air. All the while I continued to monitor the hiring practices of the highway patrol and they weren't getting any better.

March of 2004 came along and I made a slight transition in my field of work accepting a job as a Police Officer with the US Department of Veterans Affairs. For the first time in over thirteen years I was able to once again donned the uniform of the law. The uniform of regulation was midnight blue, also known in the cop world as LAPD blue. Getting back in the saddle again did not take much adjusting to. It was like I never left, but instead had been on a long vacation. I also maintained a part-time driving job with Roadway Express which had recently merged with the largest trucking company in the nation. Every cop knows you don't do this kind of work for the money which was another unremorseful reason for hanging onto my commercial driver's license. I was in high gear and things were looking good. Aviation, on the other hand, took a back seat during this restructuring phase.

During October of that year I received my fourth and last invitation to this pageant of make-believe misfits. Eleven years and two months of futile persistence, senseless patience, and a slow growing mountain of evidence that only a hungry lawyer with a late Rolls-Royce payment would love. This interview called for a different strategy, a different angle of attack. A fellow officer and prosperous friend named Tom once told me, "If you keep doing what you did you will keep getting what you got." And in light of those words of wisdom I made a few changes. The elegant three piece suit that stuck with me all those years stayed neatly pressed in the closet and was substituted by plain slacks and a short sleeve dress shirt. Not quite the Rodeo Drive attire but instead the modest department store men's section. The shinny military shoes were replaced by plain black leather which I had used on several occasions. The military buzz haircut grew about an inch and the briefcase case took the day off. So there I went to meet the latest crew of actors. Same place, same crowd. The place had not changed much in eleven years. The old highway patrol headquarters building showed no signs of improvements with its many layers of old paint. As I walked in through the main entrance it was all coming back to me as if I had just been there a few days prior. The usual greet by the same receptionist with her list of expected guests. She handed me the all too familiar information packet every applicant is asked to fill out as they anxiously wait there turn. Within a matter of minutes I had reached the last page, the page that houses the question that all candidates think will make them shine above all the rest. And the final question of the beauty pageant goes as follows. "Why do you want to be a Tennessee State Trooper?" I asked myself that same question a hundred times that day. But this time the answer was nothing like the past. I have heard trooper hopefuls answer everything - *to protect and serve, to help man kind, it's something I always wanted to do.* I was no exception to all these exquisite sales pitches but this day my answer would be a little different, a lot more honest, and much more reasonable than I had ever been before. My answer was short and sweet. In bold black letters I wrote the words: I heard you were looking for Spanish speaking officers.

The receptionist approached me and gave me the sign. It was show time and I was fired up and ready to act and so were they. Same questions, same routine, and only the faces have changed to protect the innocent. So I went up on stage and played the game until curtain time. No costume to portray a financial fake, no makeup to hide the tone of my skin, and no mask that many would use to camouflage a soon-to-be thug with a badge. My resume spoke for itself and what you saw was what you got. And as I walked out of the station that afternoon and into the parking lot I glanced towards the helipad to admire the one iron bird that was sticking half way out of the hanger. As I started my car I felt as if I had just put on an award-winning stage performance in front of an empty auditorium. I knew it was all a scam, like an old-fashion cleverly rigged Vegas slot machine. You can pull the handle all day long but you won't get a dime. A well planned game put on display to justify the highway patrol's corrupt hiring system. But what I did not know was that lurking behind stage was the governor's office quietly chipping away at one of the ties that was keeping the big tent over this circus and all it needed was the help of this soft spoken Puerto Rican to bring this big tent crashing down.

Months passed and I continued with my role of a police officer and when I was not doing that I was behind the wheel of a truck for some extra cash. Our jurisdiction covered a small area north of town and there was not much activity in the form of street action but the job was gratifying and it was certainly good for the resume. There were long night chats with the guys at the station. Three or maybe even four per shift is the most you would find at our agency. There was a lot of quiet time like many departments with a little bit of police action mixed in every now and then. I volunteered some charity work with the local Civil Air Patrol but my work schedule interfered most of the time. One night my partner Scott and I touched on the subject of corruption and the badge. That night I told him that I could never quite figure out what lead police officers to turn to a life of crime. Scott threw at me some possible reasons but even after attempting to justify the reasons I still could not comprehend the logic or reasoning behind it. Scott pointed out that police training videos covering ethics and professional responsibilities have shown that the most well-known excuses for corruption were power and money. I debated for hours telling Scott that money could not possibly be the reason because that was the one thing that law enforcement seriously lacked and if anyone accepted this job for the money then they probably had not done a fair job at looking over the hundreds of other money-making options available in today's world. I debated the power theory based on a court room visit several years back when the federal court judge threw a room full of uniformed officers out into the hallway as to prevent the intimidation of a Pro Se Plaintiff by the defense. That plaintiff was me and that memorable moment will stay in my head for years to come. I looked over at Scott and said "Now that's power." And if I wanted true power I would have become a federal court judge. I also told Scott that if I wanted money I would have vigorously pursued a career with the airlines. Scott knew he still had not sold me any valid nor understandable reason as to why a cop would walk the dark side of corruption. Maybe I will never understand why. I told Scott about the time I heard a call over my scanner years back. The call was about a Las Vegas officer attempting to investigate a complaint of an assault victim called in by a grocery store clerk. He was unable to make contact with the victim who was described as an elderly immigrant female. The neighborhood the officer was assigned to had a large immigrant population most of which were from Central and South America. He informed the dispatcher that he was unable to make contact with the victim because she was terrified of the police and left the area after the store attendant called the complaints line. So the officer had no other choice but to return to service. That heart felt but honest comment remained engraved in my mind for years to come. That clear summer night crime must have taken the night off. There was total radio silence all night and we did not get a call for the entire shift. The forum was open for debate and our late night chat went uninterrupted for hours. We covered a lot but we never could fathom why any individual would get pleasure out of making this uniform portray a sign of fear, horror, or even terrorism. I went on to tell Scott that every time I left the office and entered the public eye I checked the mirror to make sure my aviator wings displayed over my name tag were straight and level. It was a terrorist that put hundreds of pilots out of work a few years back. It even bankrupted an entire airline and took a hit to the rest. That same terrorist walked the same halls I once walked while attending a flight school in Oklahoma. He is now behind bars in Colorado's Super-max Federal Penitentiary. That's where a terrorist should be. Not wearing wings and certainly not wearing a badge.

The inactivity lasted throughout the night. As radio silence dominated the airways and with the driver's window rolled down, I looked out towards Highway 231. All you could hear were the sounds of the leaves swaying in the breeze and the locusts chirping in the distant. I glanced over at the passenger's seat and could see that slightly sticking out of my police work bag was Johnny Cochran's Journey To Justice. A book I had borrowed from the local library and one of the most motivating factors throughout this entire ordeal. A hard-copy book I had read during lunch breaks and late night reading sessions that had become an educational piece of literature and a valuable tool for this one time fool for a lawyer. I tucked it back into the bag and zipped it shut. And there I sat, one bored cop hungry for action. Many say it's a blessing in disguise. A sign of a job well done. Some even consider it being at the right place at the right time. But deep down within there is always that mysterious, guilty feeling that lingers in the back of a cop's mind reminding him that if crime is not happening there it is taking place somewhere else. And maybe that tranquil July night I was at the wrong place at the wrong time. But I wasn't the only victim at the wrong place at the wrong time that night. I later discovered that on that same night on a dark and lonely downtown street, eight hundred miles north in the small Pennsylvania town of Shenandoah a Latino immigrant out for a late night stroll found himself in the mists of a horrifying episode that would put Mississippi Burning to shame. A scene that would turn the American dream into the American nightmare and where a get-out-of-jail free card for six murder suspects would give a Las Vegas mobster a run for his money. And as he paid the ultimate price pursuing the American dream the Shenandoah Police was nowhere in sight.

And as I sat there looking across the field, watching traffic come to a halt for the night, I recalled how many years back I had considered pursuing a career as a magician in the field of entertainment. The Circus Circus Hotel was the only local hotel on The Strip that catered to minors. And it was also one of the few places where you could find a Magic Shop that would suit the needs of any aspiring magician. Every visit to the hotel called for a stop at the Magic Shop to check out the latest gadgets and an assorted array of clever devices that would intrigue the minds of curious spectators. It was a short walk from the mezzanine level of the hotel to the shop which would take me on a short journey through the main casino floor of the hotel. I would often cut right through the middle of the dingy and uninviting casino floor to knock a few seconds off of the journey. And as I did I would look down at the machines in hopes of finding a deserted coin or two. It was not long before I found myself considering an alternate route the day some arrogant nut case came out of some dark smoke filled corner and rudely ordered me off the casino floor. He looked like the typical Vegas gambler type. Like the many who roamed the floor dazzling their admirers with a credit report in their back pocket and too broke to pay attention, this lonely loser appeared to have dropped his last dime in the bucket of never-never land. Loaded with a stack of credit cards for which to charge advances made the casino cage your only friend. Too foolish to realize that the casino could care less who you were as long as you paid the ticket.

So I paid him no mind and went about my journey zigzagging my way down the busy corridor of guests and gamblers. And once at the Magic Shop I would casually browse the display racks well aware that most were quite expensive, and at my age, well beyond my financial reach. The store clerk suspected that of me after inquiring about some of the prices and soon after that began to stay clear of me the moment I entered the store. Nevertheless, there was no charge for window shopping. Like many shops and stores, it was a money machine milking you for everything you had. Years later I would learn that the best business is no business and saving your way to wealth was a sure way of achieving success. And I would also discover that this train of thought would quickly put you on the receiving end of every evil eye of every greedy profit seeker within hearing distance. I often compare this behavior to what pilots call the Region of Reverse Command. But as strange as it may sound, I have always felt that the life of a magician was not a bad way to make a living. Besides, Las Vegas was the perfect place for that line of work.

Just before the end of the shift my cell phone alerted me to a message left from earlier that evening. The call came from my Squadron Commander at the U.S. Air Force Auxiliary Civil Air Patrol. Abraham Pabon was a native of the island and had been a dedicated volunteer member with the Patrol for many years. Like any good leader who has been around for a while, Abraham is resolutely focused on getting the mission accomplished. His reputation for battling a vigorous task and being the last man standing goes a long way. Add this to holding the title as leader of choice, and you will understand the challenges he faces. Seeing him in action is far from a new concept. His determination stands out far beyond most. And when he takes command, he envelopes the stage with his dedication to duty, and does it in grand style. Pushing the envelope of expertise, his work is meant to evoke progress and success. Not to mention his devotion to family, the courage to lead, and his relentless contribution to help families and communities survive and prosper.

I took a moment to call Abraham and voiced my regrets for not being able to participate in most of the volunteer activities. I was surprise to discover that he was not particularly worried about my lack of attendance. However, he was more concerned about not having a pilot available to conduct orientation flights and Air Force assigned missions. This was a dilemma that he often expressed to me and something that I could not fathom for the longest. So I said to him "Abraham, with so many certified pilots out there I simply cannot understand how you cannot get your hands on a squadron pilot." His response that evening came to me as a wakeup call which later put to rest any questions I had in the past. He said to me "It is quite simple, nobody wants to fly for free." This news took a few seconds for me to digest and stayed on my mind for the rest of the night. Before the night was over reality had sunk in. Half a million dollars worth of equipment, courtesy of the taxpayers, and no one to fly it. It was also a reminder that a person's skills, talents, and abilities are always in demand where and when greed and prejudice serve no purpose.

I turned off my cell phone and stored it in my work bag as I felt a cool breeze blowing through the driver's side window. I began to roll the window up as the breeze blew in a few neighboring leaves. I paused for a second and looked up as the sound of a low powered piston engine aircraft caught my attention. I said to myself "The last arrival for the night." I sat there watching this straggler make his way home as he conducted a low approach to the local airport two miles south of my location. But what is done is done. I often remind myself the phrase that keeps me from turning in my badge and taking off this uniform for good. "It's just another day in this crazy world of make-believe."

On the early morning hours of December 1st of 2005 I had just returned from an eleven hour run from the City of Bristol located on the eastern edge of Tennessee. I was sitting in the driver's break room tuning out all of the usual gossip and rumors that floated around the driver's room. I was almost done updating my logbook when I heard a driver ask out loud "Hey, aren't these the guys who write us tickets?" I could not resist but to glance over to my right and watch as he looked at the front page of that morning's newspaper. He looked over it for a split second and placed it back on the table and grab his belongings and headed towards the door. Curious to see what it was he was looking at I walked over to the other side of the table and in big bold letters on the front page of the Tennessean read- *background checks flag 48 state troopers.* I could not believe my eyes. "Could this be a sign?" I asked myself. The Tennessean was actually brave and daring enough to print a negative article about what really went on inside the highway patrol. That was something you never saw. So I snatched up the headlines and headed to my car, coffee stains and all. My next stop was the nearest service station to pick up a clean and freshly printed copy of the same paper. Not only was it a souvenir but a key that would help me unlock the mystery I had been seeking. And for the weeks to follow there were headlines after endless headlines- *Tennessee Bureau of Investigation shelves THP ticket probe, Cronyism permeates THP Governor says, THP housecleaning sweeps out 2 more, Clout aided Troopers with records* ,,and the list went on and on. Now every news source in Tennessee was competing to break the ice. And the timing could not have been better.

Three weeks had passed and in the mail I received letter number four right on schedule. Not surprising. It got very little reaction out of me. I had my hands full with my personal investigation of what was turning out to be one of the most sophisticated illegal hiring practices by a state highway patrol agency in years. The governor's office was doing its part to shuffle things around under the radar and I was doing my part as a contribution to the Affirmative Action cause. In January of 2006 I continued my investigation and with a little help from my partner and friend, the Freedom of Information Act, I was able to retrieve the last few bits of statistics that would help to blow the cover off the case. To my satisfaction the stats indicated a total of 54 lucky candidates chosen for the next Trooper class and out of those 54 only two Hispanics were interviewed and one was hired. A large scale comparison showed that the state had progressed from zero to one over an eleven year period. The only mystery I had to solve now was to find out who that one Hispanic candidate was. And that was a challenge since the fifty four names on the list of the fortunate chosen candidates showed that none were bearing a traditional Spanish name.

Nevertheless, my investigation continued and as regulations stipulated I was required to allow the incompetent jokers of the EEOC 180 days to conduct an investigation prior to being granted a Notice of Right to Sue. Already familiar with their lousy operation, I knew all I had to do was to patiently wait until the end of the six months. I knew that the EEOC was notorious for not concluding its investigations within the six month period especially if they determined that there was evidence of a violation. This meant they would have to work, and they were not about to do that. On exactly the one hundred and eighty first day I contacted the EEOC to inquire about the status of the case and not to my surprise, they were still working on the case. So I requested my Notice of Right to Sue letter along with all the information and documents obtained by them in their investigation. A quick review of the EEOC logs revealed exactly what I suspected. The incompetent clowns in suits did what they do best, nothing. Case filed, case opened, and after six months of no activity case closed upon claimants request. Now armed with eleven years of statistics and the piss-poor investigative file from the EEOC the clock was ticking and I had exactly ninety days to find a lawyer and file this case in court.

I once worked with a fellow officer who years prior owned a very profitable dog training business. During a meeting with management he stated that in the business world exited two fundamental choices. Either you were productive or you were out-of-here. That's not quite the same principal in government service. The civil service mentality is not fond of the word change and a guaranteed salary is a daily reminder that regardless of productivity Uncle Sam would send you a check. As for the old school, that's just the way they want to keep it.

As for me, let's just say I did not share the ways of the old school. My unsolicited proverbial saying "Out with the old and in with the new" put me on the receiving side of numerous evil looks often too numerous to count. Times were changing and the brave and bold crowd spear-heading this change had to be prepared to endure a tough battle. As the days went by I became more and more convinced that there weren't too many warriors up for the fight. It was looking dimmer and dimmer by the minute. All avenues were leading to dead ends and there was only one conclusion. Even to my surprise, it was looking like there was only one person cut out for the job of navigating this vessel through the storm. Every pilot knows the halfway point is the point of no return. It's just a matter of riding out the waves and hoping to make it out in one piece on the other side.

Sometimes the only volunteer is not the one who steps forward but the only one who does not take a step back. That being the case, I found myself unofficially designated as the only one fit to do the job. And in this crazy world of make believe, it sometimes helps to pull out some Las Vegas style magic tricks from out of the hat.

CHAPTER FOUR

The Case

Years in the military taught me a few things about law enforcement. It also taught me that good investigative skills range from seeking out evidence, preserving the crime scene, and most important safe-keeping its content. The next step was presenting it to the court. It was time for me to test my skills. And that I did.

In January of 1994 shortly after the selection of the fortunate candidates my suspicion led me to ask questions. I requested a statistical breakdown reflecting all ethnic groups and genders with the assistance of the Jurisdiction of the Freedom of Information Act. In a sense I was policing the hiring practices of the Department of Safety. It was the beginning of an indisputable fourteen year paper trail of the injustices and corruptness of the administrative staff of the Department of Safety and it all came in handy during the discovery phase. This information would be as good as gold in the years to come and with that in mind I continued to monitor their hiring practices throughout the years. The abundance of documented evidence also brought amazement to the few spineless lawyers who I managed to consult with about the case and even impressed the Magistrate judge.

The incompetent bozos of the EEOC had issued me a "Notice of Right to Sue," which by law was good for 90 days and I knew I had to get busy. Although my good friend Mario specialized in Immigration Law, he knew a few lawyers in town who dealt with

Employment Law so he referred me their way. The very first one was an older gentleman by the name of Edward. He claimed to have been in the business for over thirty five years. I will say I was impressed and with thirty five years under your belt you can't get any better than that. I thought I was talking to the best of the best and I could not wait to get started. He sat back in his plush leather chair, pulled out a notepad and began to ask me questions about my record and so on. I really did not see the need to emphasize on my record, besides I was not the defendant so I chose to save this intriguing man some time and handed him my well-maintained evidence packet. He looked at the stack and as he flipped through the documents and glanced at the dates I could see the expression on his face. He then looked at me as somewhat stunned and said "This is great!" Fourteen years of collected and well preserved evidence was more than great but I just took the compliment and left it in the hands of the pros. He said he would look it over and get back in touch with me. With the clock ticking I patiently waited to hear word and approximately one week after that afternoon meeting I received my packet of evidence in the mail with a letter which stated something along the lines of-*I don't think I am good enough for this case. Good luck in your search for justice.* I could not understand what had happened. "Some best of the best" I said to myself. The next day I called Mario and with only sixty days left he assured me that lawyers were a dime a dozen. And he was right, but getting them to except such a case was a different story. A few weeks later I got a call from Mario asking me to stop by his office to meet another candidate by the name of David. I sat quietly as Mario introduced me to this man. They briefly talked about the good old days and a few other things. The guest lawyer shifted the conversation by proudly boasting of his daughter who had just obtained her Private Pilot's license. This got my attention so I heard the man out. He went on to say the one thing about lawyers that is all so true. He raised his right hand and pointed his index finger towards the sky and said "I believe ninety-nine percent of all lawyers are paper pushers and only one percent will truly fight for your case and I consider myself in that one percent." This is the man for the job I thought to myself. I looked at Mario thinking to myself this might be the guy we have been looking for. Mario asked me to explain to him the whole nine yards so I decided to start off on a good note. The one thing that might trigger some interest since his daughter just got through getting her pilot's license. So I began by clarifying that the issue at stack revolved around just a few things to include a pilot's license. To be a little more specific, my pilot's license. He looked puzzled at first and as the story went deeper into detail his eyes got wider and wider. His eyes swept across the table as I presented the evidence in perfect chronological order displaying each and every document perfectly intact in its sheet protector. And as the mystery unraveled, he quickly discovered he was no longer in that one percent. When I mentioned the defendant as the Tennessee Department or Safety the man looked like he had just seen a ghost. Mario jumped in to point out how the stats indicated large numbers of Hispanic applicants scoring in the top ten and zero being considered for the Trooper position. The breakdown, the policies, the numbers and percentages, it was all overwhelming. As Mario expressed his disbelief with the stats I sat there watching his every expression. He wanted no part of this and his only concern right then and there was the nearest exit. Mario never caught it but I did and I decided to save him the unnecessary grief and cut him loose. He told Mario he would look over the evidence in detail and talk to his firm. I told him that if by some strange chance they decide that they would not take the case to please mail me the evidence back. He tore out of the office like a bat out of hell. I looked over at Mario and said "by the looks on his face I can tell you he is not going to take this case." Mario wanted me to think positively but I was more than positive that it would be the last time we would see that cat. So much for one percent and three weeks later I received my packet in the mail with a very well written letter stating something along the lines as *–considering the circumstances we will not be able to financially support this case.* It ended with the usual good luck. I was grateful that he at the least had the decency to return my paperwork and from that day on I referred to these lawyers as the ninety-nine percenters. The clock was still ticking away and now I was down to forty five days, no thanks to these cowards, so we kept hammering away. Lawyers came and lawyers went. It was like trying to find a needle in a hay stack. Not far down the road I was referred to another candidate by the name of Jerry who Mario had worked with sometime in the past. The Nashville Scene did an article on him in the recent years. The Scene, as most locals called it, was a bit controversial but yet a straight forward and free speaking local paper that held nothing back. Whether fact or false they did not care. They would print it and the people would buy it. One night while on the Internet I came upon his article and with time on my hands I read through it as it described him as the biggest jerk on the Nashville Bar Association, but in more vulgar terms. I gave him a call and from the get-go his rude and obnoxious demeanor clearly verified everything The Scene described him as quite well but I often wondered just how much of it was hyped-up as a publicity scheme. Some described him as a hard-core lawyer looking after the best interest of the immigrant community. The Scene described him as an ex-secret service agent turned lawyer utilizing a belligerent jerk-like demeanor in which to get his point across. Either way he did not impress me but I gave him a chance. And after a short conversation and an exchange of facts, it appeared that this clown was more interested in criticizing my timely delay in seeking his services than taking on the case. Needless to say, I never heard back from him.

Names came and went. Friends, co-workers, community activists, you name it. I had names and numbers coming at me from all directions. The Legal Aid Society who was quick to point out the list of cases they did not handle, Pro Bono lawyers who were mostly non-existent, and the list went on and on. There were numerous phony non-profit organizations which were quick to point out the types of cases or services to the public which they did not handle. Even the Puerto Rico Legal Defense and Education Fund who I had generously donated my hard working money to throughout my short military career did not waste any time in turning their backs on a Persian Gulf War era veteran.

Day after day, week after week, time was running out and so were my options. I was getting dangerously close to the 90th day and Mario's list of referrals was all dried up. It was looking like there would be no other alternative but to file as a Pro Se which in non-legal terms meant you were representing yourself in court. It was also known as the fool for a lawyer. But I was about to give the term fool a whole new meaning.

The Equal Employment Opportunity Commission was out of the question which turned out to be a blessing in disguise and there weren't anymore government agencies to choose from. But one day while having lunch with a friend he mentioned the office of Tennessee Human Rights Commission along with the name of a guy named Frank who was said to be the only Hispanic and the only Spanish speaking staff member on the payroll. My past experiences in interacting with Hispanic or even minority sources that were devoted to making changes for the better and improving crucial issues that affect historically disadvantaged groups were always advantageous to the cause, except when you ran into a racist who targeted his own people. And every now and then I would find myself sharing the road with many of them.

The THRC, as some called it, was the stateside version of EEOC. Infested with a lot of the similarities held by their federal counterpart to include their bogus claims of seeking justice for victims of discrimination, their slow investigative times, and extremely week and lenient fines and senseless remedies. Equipped with secretaries baring investigator titles, it did not take long to discover that this incompetent army of clowns would make the Keystone Cops look like Delta Force. With nothing to lose I picked up the phone and went to work. After a short introduction and the name of the referral I gave him a brief synopsis of the case and a run-down of what I was looking for. My suspicion was correct as this ringmaster slowly accelerated down a highway of horse manure. He was quick to fire off his trumped up resume. High on himself and with very little to offer, all he could say was "You need to get a lawyer." It appeared as if the state ethics board was unaware of this agency's common practice of promoting private business with the public's hard earned tax dollars, or maybe they were. When it came to the state, nothing surprised me. It was the same song and dance as all those before him. I informed him of my unsuccessful attempts of obtaining an attorney. His only response in a rather rude tone, “Well, do you have any money?” I informed the man of my role as a Pro Se along with my challenging task and the need to research similar cases. It was clear that the only service this joker was going to render was his words of a fool which he fired off like a machine gun. *Well, that's just going to tick-off the lawyers and judges...I've gone all the way up to the Supreme Court and I would hate to be in your shoes, I feel for you.* The baloney spilled over like a volcano. If I had not been wearing my boots that day I would still be washing the horse manure off my feet. And with only days left I prepared for my last option.

One March afternoon with only one day left to file and just minutes before the court clerk's office closed I arrived at federal court to file the initial complaint. A modest fee of $250 is all they asked. An amount well invested. The next morning I showed up at the Highway Patrol headquarters near downtown to personally serve the Commissioner with the Summons to Appear in Court. It was an awesome feeling and a historical moment at that. I was the first Hispanic in the history of the state of Tennessee to file a suit of this nature. It was also the beginning of change, a symbol of power, and a symbol of hope. It had been several years since I had walked this similar path but it was all coming back to me. Most lawyers charge an arm and a leg to serve a defendant and many even forget to serve the papers causing an unnecessary delay and an embarrassing start. But for me two dollars in unleaded fuel is all it took.

That same week Mario gave me the name of a reporter named Bonna who worked with the Tennessean. The Tennessean was the largest statewide newspaper and after several failed attempts to contact the reporter who covered the background checks and all the recent scandals and surfacing administrative blunders of the Department of Safety I came to the conclusion that racial discrimination in the highway patrol's recruiting department was one topic too hot for even him to handle. I hesitated but after giving it some thought I went ahead with the call, but this time the call was made to Bonna. She seemed interested from the instant I mention the suit. She took some notes and immediately called me back for the rest of the details concerning the case. There was one question that caught me off guard. She asked me "What do think about the Kroll Report?" I explained to her that I knew nothing about this report and doing so she recommended that I look into it because it contained similar issues relating to the suit I had just filed in court. It was almost as if she had given me a hint, a sign. And that it was. The following week news articles and television stations were reporting on details that resulted from this Kroll Report. I went one step further by looking into the Internet to see what it was that I could find. It appeared that the governor's office had begun a discrete investigation of the internal problems of the Department of Safety and highway patrol. The news about the wide spread corruption had reached a point which even the governor's office could no longer ignore. With the media hounding at the door of Capitol Hill the governor's only option was to take administrative action and it did so by hiring a private consulting firm out of New York to look into the controversial matters of the infested highway patrol and to have a report on his desk ASAP. That's when the Kroll Consulting Services stepped into the picture and the results were open to the public. However, this only covered the administrative side of the sickness but did nothing for the victims affected by the crime.

My investigative skills were paying off and I managed to obtain a copy of all fifty pages of the report and it described everything just as I had suspected all along. It also gave me an idea as to what to look for in my investigation and with the discovery phase soon approaching I had to have my ducks in a row. Articles by the Tennessean kept surfacing but very little covering the topic of racial discrimination in the realm of hiring and how it had impacted Hispanics and other minorities. An uncomfortable topic most people in this day and age chose to avoid or overlook.

From the beginning the defense began to play their legal games which were quickly shot down by the court. The case was assigned to a young attorney from the Attorney General's office named Michael and they wasted no time trying to move the case out of Federal Court and into the state but the federal court judge was not about to let that happen. Court judges often knew the challenges Pro Se litigates were up against and were well aware of the unethical nature of lawyers concerning civil rights cases and this judge was no exception. It was a nice try but the court would not go for it and the court was quick to get rolling. There was no hearing to determine if the case was frivolous. This was an indication that the judge had a good feeling about the case and quickly moved forward to the discovery phase. The discovery phase was set to be complete by August 25th of 2006. I received the scheduling order marking the deadline for the conclusion of the discovery phase and here is where the fun began.

The first thing on the agenda was a deposition and I received instructions to appear at the Polk building for a deposition scheduled to last the entire day and to exceed beyond. I knew that every good lawyer did his homework and seeing that I was the only good lawyer for the job I got to doing mine. I routinely studied the Federal Rules of Civil Procedure along with the local rules of the court and as a result of knowing the rules I elected not to appear. Michael filed a motion to dismiss for my failure to attend the deposition and I found myself in front of the judge answering questions. The hearing was scheduled for September 21st at nine in the morning. The judge entered the courtroom as the bailiff ordered the court to rise. He quickly reviewed the motions and asked me why I had not attended my deposition. So I informed him that the law was quite clear and in accordance to the Federal Rules of Civil Procedure the plaintiff is obligated to a maximum of seven hours of a deposition and nothing more. The judge looked at Michael and after calling his name said "He's right." The words were music to my ears. A job well done and off to an impressive start. Both sides argued about what they wanted the judge to do. I wanted my documents and so did he. Out of fairness to the defense the judge granted Michael his requested and I was ordered to provide him with the answers to his list of interrogatory questions which he was seeking but just before Judge Bryant excused the parties I had to make one final request. I informed the judge that I had not received any of the documents I had requested and he looked over at Michael and asked "Is that correct?" Michael answered "yes" and gave his reason for withholding the papers. The judge told him that if he wanted his documents it was only fair that I should get mine. That turned out to be a second blow to the defense. Two on the first day of court, that's not good. The order was not something that the defense wanted to hear. The judge gave both parties less than thirty days to obtain from the other what each side wanted.

October came along and I noticed there was still something unusual, something the state was trying so desperately to hold back. I began to suspect that the defense was catching on to my strategy and knew that relinquishing this information could be damaging to the defense and they were not about to release that evidence without throwing a few legal tricks.

On October the 16th I filed a motion to compel informing the court that I had not received the documentation I had been waiting for. I informed the court that the plaintiff reserved the right to illustrate how he and other minority groups were treated different than the other applicants and to prove his point along with his qualifications this set of information was crucial. Criminal, drug, and juvenile records where not except from discovery.

The defense responded in opposition arguing that it had fully responded to the plaintiff's request for production of documents and that the plaintiff was now seeking additional documents that were beyond the scope of his original request. It was a good argument but the court responded "with due consideration to the plaintiff's Pro Se litigation, the court liberally construes the language of his document request to included these documents, It is so ORDERED." This gave the defense thirty days to comply.

Not only was I pleased with the courts consideration for my Pro Se status but further amazed as to the simplicity of the legal process. I was still having a hard time believing what I was doing and where I was going. All the warnings and unsolicited lectures of people telling me that I was attempting to do the impossible did not seem so impossible, if anything it appeared amazingly practical and incredibly feasible.

After reviewing the information sent by the defense I was stunned to discover that the documentation sent by them was a copy of what they had sent earlier and clearly a ploy to avoid relinquishing the only piece of evidence they were trying so desperately to hold back. I was outraged and on June 28th I made a surprising move by filing a Motion for Entry of Default Judgment. I argued that the defense made perfectly clear in previous memorandums that what they had sent earlier during that period of the discovery was all the documentation they intended to release. I further argued that the defense had failed to plead or otherwise defend this action and that the Plaintiff was entitled to judgment by default. I added an impressive touch further stating "Pursuant to the Federal Rules of Civil Procedure this court is empowered to enter a default judgment against the defendant for relief sought by the plaintiff in its complaint." An added touch I was certain would get their attention and get results. And it worked like a charm. The court agreed and sent out the order giving the defense fifteen days to cough up the evidence or cough up the cash. Their response was quite arrogant in the sense that they argued that although Pro Se litigants are afforded leeway, those who proceed without counsel, in other words an attorney, must still comply with the procedural rules that govern civil cases, that the plaintiff was failing to comply not due to willfulness, bad faith or fault, and that the relief sought was inappropriate. The one thing that every lawyer hates with a passion is a court's merciful ways towards a Pro Se. The defense stomped their feet, pouted, moped, cried, and flopped on the floor like a fish out of water. What a bunch of babies- I thought to myself. Besides, the court order was clear and all the whining in the world would not convince the court to retract its decision. I felt as if the court was going out of its way to make my legal journey as obstacle free as possible.

I was beginning to get used to the life of a lawyer. A good one that is. Researching court procedures was almost second nature and filing was something a five year old on his way to the ice cream shop could do. An occasional visit to the federal court house was all it took and filing at the court clerk's office was free of charge. A dollar for the parking meter and some loose change for gas is all the money this lawyer needed. And if I wasn't in the mood for the trip downtown the U.S. Post Office would do the work for me." How easy could it get?" I asked myself.

I will admit that I had a temporary setback or two. My first Motion for Summary Judgment was denied do to a typing error which even had the judge baffled. The court ruled in favor of the defense and recommended the case be dismissed based solely on an affidavit signed by the Human Resources Director for the Tennessee Department of Safety. Kerri had held the position since April of 2003. The sworn affidavit stated that my relatively low interview score was the sole reason for my disqualification. Accepting defeat camc hard. But it was the thought that counted and the willingness to try that deserved some credit. The defense celebrated but the victory was short lived. My motivation level dropped into the negative range and I could not sleep that night. I tossed and turned outraged at the justice system. I was convinced Affirmative Action was dead. The following morning I read over the court's recommendation for dismissal. I stared at it for hours in disbelief. Trying to convince myself that it wasn't over yet, I tried so hard looking for something, anything. I asked the lord for a sign and after an hour of fixation I realized that I had the answer that I was looking for in front of me all along. The court's order and recommendation clearly stated that the defendant was reluctant to hire the plaintiff for a Trooper position when his true interest was in Aviation. The ball was in my court and the only way to survive was to prove this statement wrong. The order and recommendation also read "According to the Human Resources Director's memorandum, the plaintiff was not hired because his interview score was lower than all of the other applicants in the Nashville District." This shifted the burden of proof to me and now it was up to me to offer evidence that this proffered reason was pretextual, or in other words, a fabricated excuse to conceal the truth. A voice told me to review all the latest documents that Michael had sent me. So I did and to my amazement I came upon a valuable piece of evidence in the form of an application submitted by one of the recruits. On the very top of the first page of that particular piece of evidence were instructions made to the human resources office. The instructions were to deliver with priority via inter-departmental mail. As I wondered why the priority and what was so special about this applicant form that had to stick out above the rest I continued to flip through the pages and on the second page I saw the words in clear print: SEEKING HELICOPTER PILOT POSITION. I continued to flip through the pages and on the very last page was a photo copy of the applicant's pilot's license along with a copy of his flight physical. Credentials only a pilot would recognize. I looked up at the ceiling and said "Thank you lord." And that was not the only sign. I started to look through all the papers with a fine-tooth comb. The negligence and the incompetence that was cultivating in Kerri's office along with the help of the rest of the administrative staff and this rag-tag gang of political thugs turned out to work more and more in my favor by the minute. Pieces of evidence were pouring down on me like a waterfall. A close investigation of the applicant scores indicated that I was not the lowest in the Nashville district like the defense had informed the court. Instead, it indicated that there were five others whose scores were much lower than mine. And to make matters worse two were hired and sent on to the academy. I was astonished as to the ineptness of the defense but at the same time delighted as to what I had discovered. I asked myself "How could the defense fail to notice such damaging evidence, or did their arrogance simply overshadow their litigation skills?" Nevertheless, it didn't benefit me any to try and figure that one out. It was then that I understood why the defense tried so hard to hold back this crucial piece of information. I finally found the smoking gun and I did not hesitate to inform the judge of this newly discovered evidence.

On September 7th I set foot back in ring. I filed my objection to the court's recommendation arguing that I had recently received and reviewed new evidence but the court still denied it. I pressed on arguing that the Rules of Civil Procedure stipulate that both parties should be given ample opportunity to present all available evidence. I knew it was a long shot. I tried a different approach with this argument. This time I included the evidence. The same evidence the defense tried desperately to withhold. The worst the court could do was to glance over it and toss it in the trash. But it was a chance I was willing to take.

In the mean time the court had issued a status conference for September the 21st and I once again found myself in front of the judge. To my surprise Michael had chosen to bring the long anticipated documentation with him to court that morning. The interview test results neatly packed in perfect order. The judge entered the courtroom and the first question that morning was addressed to me. The judge looked over at me and asked "Have you received the documents that you had asked for?" I then answered "Yes your honor." He then asked if I had looked over them to ensure that it was in fact what I had been expecting all along. I informed him that they were brought in by the defense only minutes prior to the judge entering the courtroom. The judge generously gave me an additional four weeks to review them and file a response. Just before dismissing the court I took advantage of the opportunity to ask the judge one final request. I inquired about a statement he made in reference to appointing counsel for the plaintiff. The judge was convinced that I was doing an excellent job in representing myself that he complimented my work but felt that I was not financially broke and that appointment of counsel by the court was not necessary. I will say that I was flattered by the compliment but was becoming somewhat exhausted and could have used one either way.

After taking the time to review each and every page it was obvious to me that the format was so subjective that it had the words SCAM written all over it. With the right words you were sure to score high above the rest and you were in. Rigged like an old-fashion Vegas slot machine. You could pull the handle all day long but no jackpot. You were in or out way before you set foot in the interview room. But the evidence that really counted was in front of me all along. And thanks to the lousy work of the HR department and the arrogance of the AG's office, their most valuable piece of supporting evidence was one that would close their fate.

I spend days searching out anything that could be used as ammunition looking everything over with a microscope. The deception was pitiful. Prior criminal records weren't an obstacle, political figures named as references, and numerous background investigations returned with check marks in the blocks indicating: NOT RECOMMENDED FOR HIRE which were marked over and later changed to recommended for hire. And all the hours I spent looking and search through records for that one Hispanic applicant fortunate to enter the doors of this brothel went squandered only to find out that I had passed over his name a thousand times. Looking for traditional Spanish names was a waste of time since that one lucky dice roll had a name as Anglo as American pie. Hispanics could kiss affirmative action good bye. The only affirmative action that might get you in these doors was cold hard cash. And even that was a gamble. There was a wide gap between honesty and ruthlessness. Most honest and dedicated Troopers at low and mid level clearly opposed the indiscriminate hiring practices but the evidence clearly showed the few that unremorsefully played on this large-scale discrimination and corruption. With the evidence in hand and the few bits and pieces of information that still surfaced from the Tennessean, I was able to put together a well organized display of exhibits to present during trial. The Kroll report was helpful and the newspaper's recent story of paying your way into the highway patrol with donations to various political parties was a sure way in. Most referred did not even know the person who used their name as reference to obtain a leading edge and some even disapproved but it was too late. The door was opened and they were in. Some political donations, whether true or not, were as low as $500 and some went as high as five times that amount. It almost seemed as if they were running a brothel of low budget prostitutes on the Las Vegas Strip. Cash and names were the most appropriate tool at this table accompanied with a dice roll where the rules did not transmit neatly in black and white, but instead shades of gray and where a Hispanic did not stand a chance. Any doughts or restrictions about your physical state were kicked to the side and it showed as extremely overweight men and women in uniform patrolled the streets. I recalled standing in line at a community center and over-hearing an older couple standing in front of me discretely comment on a small town cop who was standing in full uniform a short distance away. The elderly couple described her as not being in the best physical shape. She had rolls every which way but loose and would make the Michelin man look like a Vegas show girl. As for civilian personnel in many departments, they were never in the public eye and most were in even worse physical shape.

Certain names as a references had you wearing a badge and a uniform overnight. The more I researched the more I discovered that the mountain of evidence continued to grow as I watched as the tent came crashing down on this inner circle of misfits. The Department of Safety and top officials of the highway patrol made a Colombian drug cartel look like school girls. The defense knew that now I held the deck of cards and I was ready to get back in the ring swinging. The fact that they are a defeated regime, collectively and individually, must be impressed upon them that they will hesitate to continue this conduct of illegal discrimination. It was just a matter or time.

On Oct 8, 2007 I informed the court of the newly discovered evidence which included the prioritized employment application from the applicant seeking the pilot's position. The details of the evidence also included demonstrated to the court that the affidavit provided by Kerri and its allegations of the plaintiff's score being the lowest of all was clearly false. Armed with a mountain of evidence I reminded the court, just like the landmark case of Burdines, I produced genuine issues of material fact showing that the proffered reason was not the true reason for the employment decision, and that race was. I further argued that the plaintiff had once again met his burden of proof. This was a devastating blow to the defense and on that Friday just before the court clerk's office closed its doors for the day the defense sent an urgent fax to the court with a revised copy of Kerri's previous affidavit. This Affidavit made an embarrassing statement indicating that the previous affidavit submitted by the defense alleging that the plaintiff was not hired because he scored lower than all the others was "imprecise." The proffered reason this time was even more absurd and made very little logic compared to the previous. And throughout the months objections were fired off by both sides. Motions came and went and as they did I caught onto the fact that the defense was avoiding rebutting or even commenting on the three key pieces of evidence at hand. Those pieces of evidence were the helicopter pilot's application, the score sheet, and the only Hispanic applicant chosen by the defense. All were what the court considered presumable assumptions and all required an explanation but the defense dodged the bullet to all ends. The defense stood their ground and never once commented on the hiring of the pilot. Even worse, the hiring of those not recommended for hire by the highly respected and exceptionally hard-working background investigators confirmed that prior criminal records prioritized hiring over minority groups with impeccable records and every mention of this had the defense sweating like a marathon runner in the Mojave Desert. I quickly discovered that these items would be the first on the list to drop the bombshell during trial. Three times I demanded an explanation and three times they avoided commenting at all cost. It reminded me of a broke con-artist bluffing his way through a dead-end game of blackjack. I was not in any hurry and demanded answers through the court even if it caused the case any added delay. I knew that with this evidence in hand trial would be a breeze. It was my bar B-Q and it tasted excellent. Efforts were hopeless but I think the court got the hint.

Months went by and on March 21st of 2008 the court had enough. After strenuously arguing the evidence, the court filed its

Memorandum and Order chastising the imprecise affidavit along with counsel who prepared it. The court further scrutinized the defense's ineffectiveness stating that such actions destroy the heart of the case. The court also concluded "that the plaintiff has raised a sufficient material fact for trial as pretext." It went on to say "the defense's failure to counter the plaintiff's explanation that the defense required a pilot to become a trooper first." I continued to read with delight "The court found that the defendant's shifting explanation for why the plaintiff was not hired were evidence of pretext that created a genuine issue of material fact for trial as to whether the defendant discriminated against the plaintiff in violation of Title VII of the Civil Rights Act of 1964. Therefore, the recommendation to dismiss the plaintiff's claim is hereby denied and the claim will go to trial." I looked up at the heavens and said "Thank you lord all mighty." The moment of truth had come and the defense's luck had run dry. They were all out of cards and the table was closed. Hearing the word trial was like hearing the sweet sound of victory and all that was left was the day of the trial.

Now, I did fail in the claim of Disparate Impact which met that I could not fight for or represent the various minority groups affected in the matter. However, I was successful in the Disparate Treatment claim enabling me to carry the case in defense of myself. Being blessed with this outcome I decided to go forward with it. It was better than nothing at all. The days that followed felt like the silence before the storm and the defense knew the game was all over. There was no evidence to taint, no motions to stall, no firm to financially drain, no witnesses to scare, and most important no lawyer to bribe. Now I was calling the shots and as far as I was concerned this case was going to trial and nothing was stopping it. But the sound of victory didn't sound all that loud and the media was still no where in sight. The messages left at the newsrooms were never returned. Even the local television reporter who covered Hispanic community affairs was in the loop but she never returned a call. It was as if they knew exactly who I was and about the case. They were not about to say a word and were purposely avoiding response hoping I would give up and go away. And eventually I did.

A few years back during my military days my unit was conducting a training mission just north of Frankfurt. It was close to sunset and the evening was chilly. I was chosen to play the roll of an injured soldier and the rest of my group was assigned the task of finding me and returning me to safety. I remember jumping in the Hummer and being taken a few miles up the road where my squad leader found the coordinates of the planned rescue site. I was dropped off and told to wait for the rescuing unit to arrive. As they left the area I watched as the taillights of the Hummer disappeared into the horizon. I looked around and could see nothing but wilderness. It was then that I realized that there was not a soul for miles. So I picked out a semi-cubby hole along side a large downed tree and made myself comfortable. The sun was just over the horizon and within minutes it was gone. Then there was nothing but complete darkness. I sat there bored and extremely tired from all of the earlier military exercises. My eyes were shutting as I struggled to stay awake. I was not able to keep up the struggle and dozed off in the middle of nowhere. When I awoke it was still pitch dark and I looked at my watch not realizing what had happened. I looked around and nothing. All I heard was the sound of the light breeze and the shifting leaves. I sat there helplessly waiting for a sign of life and after an hour I saw lights in the distant. As they came closer and as it did I began to hear the voice of my squad leader calling my name. The darkness went on for miles and he was not able to see me within the ocean of trees and vegetation so I turned on my flashlight and pointed it his way. When he spotted the light the Hummer came closer and he stuck his head out the window and yelled "Get in!" I jumped in the back seat and asked him what had happened. He stated that he did not know and that minutes earlier he and his driver were walking in the wilderness just outside the campsite and heard a small stampede of animals at close proximity to them. They could not see a thing because of the darkness but my squad leader suspected it was a pack of wild boars that were known to roam in this part of the wilderness. He said that the both of them froze still and waited until the noise of the herd had passed. He said "I could not see them but I could sense that they were within fifteen feet of us. All I could do was pull out my knife and hope for the best." And that's what he did until the noise dissipated and when it did they made a run for it straight to the site. When they got there they told the rest of the guys about the wild boars and to use caution while roaming in the woods. He also noticed that within the group were the guys assigned the task of search and rescue. He also noticed that I was not in the group. Right about that time the platoon sergeant approached everyone to see how the exercise turned out. The squad leader asked everyone there "Where is Laureano?" They looked at him and said "We could not find him so we just came back." That's when he realized that I was still in the woods in the fine company of wild boars. That's when they jumped in the Hummer and headed out. He asked me if I had seen the boars. I said to him "With pitch darkness, I had a hard time keeping my eyes open and dozed off. If they saw me, they probably weren't all that hungry because I am still here."

When we pulled up to the site, we jumped out of the Hummer, and all three of us headed to the formation in the center of the site for debriefing. And it wasn't good. The platoon sergeant reamed everyone in the search party. He made it clear that if you were sent out to recover a downed soldier, you did everything in your power to find that soldier, sailor, airman, or marine. That was your mission and the mission must be accomplished. He said " You find him or you don't come back until you do. Coming back empty handed is unacceptable!" The group got so quiet that you could hear a pin drop. It was that day that I learned the importance and the meaning of MISSION COMPLETE.

The days after the court's ruling were somewhat relaxing but I felt like a professional gambler eighty sixed from a casino. I felt as if I had been black-balled. It was as if the role of counsel had consumed me and I was urging for more. I was glad to have prevailed in the stages prior to trial but with nothing to investigate and no motions to file, I felt as if time stood still. I became so good at what I was doing that to stop on a dime made me feel useless. I eventually convinced myself that the role of attorney was not my profession and that this was only a one time thing soon to be over. And for just a split moment I regretted the routes I had taken and made into careers. But it was too late as far as I was concerned. Law school takes along time and I am not about to wait eight to twelve years to do what I can do now. Even at times I can't believe what I have accomplished without one day of training or schooling in the field of litigation. "What an overpriced racket." I said to myself. To think people paid good money for this type of service was saddening. But what's done is done and the only thing left was to wait.

One April evening I met up with another long-time friend at our favorite coffee shop on the east side of the City of Murfreesboro. Benito was a professional framer and drywall installer with years of experience. We often talked about going into business together. He had the expertise of a framer and I had a talent for remodeling with a touch of luxury. He was more business oriented with long-term goals of a profitable and growing business and I had an interest in turning old and run-down things into new. Money did not mean much to me but instead the final product of a job well done.

The coffee shop franchise was the largest in the nation and the brands they served had an exquisite taste to them. I'm not much of a coffee drinker but I admire its fine taste and the pleasant atmosphere this location provided its customers. The night was clear with a light breeze from the north so we sat outside in the patio area listening to the traffic and activity of this steady growing commercial district. Benito was in the middle of a divorce and I started the conversation by asking how the legal progress was going. I had an idea what to expect as an answer but I did not want to come across rude or inappropriate so I asked in the most pleasant form I could. He stated that it was at a stand still. I asked him if he wouldn't mind me asking the reason for the delay. He went on to explain that his attorney had stopped in his tracks because he needed two thousand more dollars in addition to what he was already given. Benito said "I already gave him close to two thousand when I first hired him." I was not the least bit surprised. I asked him "Have you ever thought about doing the case yourself?" He looked at me as if I was nuts. My suggestion to him was to refrain from sending this lawyer another dime and to type up a letter of termination and send it to him certified mail. He knew he did not have the least bit understanding of the court system and he was not even going to consider trying. He knew I had the know-how and experience and he asked me for some help. I started to guide him through the steps but he was busy running a small contracting business and had little time left for extra activities.

We chatted for about two hours and the subject shifted towards my pending suit. I told him things were working out like a charm. It was just another day at the office for me but there was one thing that all these years had me in a state of disbelief. One thing I could not figure out for the life of me. I looked over at Benito and said "Maybe you can figure this one out." I went on to explain "I have managed to do what the common public considers to be the impossible. I am the only person to take legal action as a result of the governor's findings of widespread corruption, cronyism, and discrimination. I am representing myself in a case where the end result stands to gain close to a million dollars in compensation for damages, if not more. I am the first Hispanic in the history of this state to file suit against an agency of this kind. And I am the first Hispanic in the history of this state to have achieved receiving a trial date. But yet there is no sight of the media. No newsroom reporters or news magazines asking for details. The number of lawyers that chickened out were too numerous to count. And the most incomprehensible part of this entire matter is that I am not interested in a dime. Money does not mean anything to me. A guilty plead is enough to satisfy me and bring this case to a close." Benito looked at me and said "I might be able to answer that." He asked me to sit back and think about the matter at stake. He asked me to put myself in everyone else's shoes and look at it from their point of view. He went on to say " With all the anti-Hispanic rhetoric going around and for the fact that you just made every lawyer within miles look like a bunch of useless paper-pushers, you can forget the local media praising this story. Furthermore, there may be a lot of money to be made on this case but if it's not a small business with a small portion of its net profits available for the taking or an easy target that involves little to no work, no lawyer is going to take your case. Besides, Hispanics have no voice in this area and the media could care less." He ended the conversation by asking me "Why are you putting all this time and energy into this?" I answered "It's my contribution to the cause and my ability to make a change for the better." He said to me "You might be fighting this case for a very long time." My answer to him was "That's alright. I am in no hurry, besides, I have always wanted to visit the Supreme Court." We talked for a few more minutes. I told him about the time the American Airline CEO said during a TV interview "The only people that benefit from bankruptcies are the lawyers." He went on to tell the viewers that when he took over the company there was a dramatic change in the profitability of his airline. I also shared with him how amazed I was at the judge's consideration for my Pro Se status. I said to him "Judges know just how bad the lawyers and law firms have manipulated the system and how it has been turned into an over-priced racket. Maybe that's why they are making it so easy for me." Benito answered "Maybe."

Ten o'clock came around and the staff began turning off the lights. That was our sign that it was time to leave. I headed towards my car and he headed to his and just before he opened the driver's door I looked over at him and said to him "Hey Benito, as for Hispanics not having a voice, well they do now." The conversation was good like always and I met up a few more times that month to update Benito on the case. The weeks to come remained fairly quiet and since the motions were done I made the best of my off time.

I made another attempt at notifying and updating the Puerto Rico Legal Defense and Education Fund and updated the Media Relations rep on the case. I informed her that I had accomplished what even they were incapable of doing. I had baked the cake and all they had to do was put the icing on top and take part of the credit. She took some notes and said she would pass it on and not to my surprise she never called back. The following day I said to myself, "If I were in their shoes I would be feeling so stupid and useless right now that I would not call back either." Understanding of the circumstances I continued on. I had heard that the Mexican American Legal Defense and Education Fund had an office in Atlanta and were very familiar with the injustices that occurred in the region. I gave them a call and they had an entirely different reaction than our Puerto Rican counterpart. They were fascinated with the results and asked me to keep them posted every step of the way until trial. They were very supportive and referred me to some helpful Spanish media sources. The gentleman who answered the phone was extremely sociable and we talked for almost an hour sharing notes and experiences relating to the matter at hand. After finishing the conversation I said to myself, "If I had only known about them during my military years I would have donated my money to them and told PRLDEF to go to the Caribe Hilton."

The following week I pulled into a Latin market in the town of Smyrna to pick up some South American food products. As I passed the news rack I grabbed and looked over some of the area's Spanish language newspapers. I had purchased some pastries and stopped for a short conversation with the cashier at the counter. I also made it a point to stop in at all of the area Spanish markets. Public relations and interaction with the community is a valuable tool used by most law enforcement agencies. However, Hispanic markets were always left out of the loop and even the few local Spanish speaking or Hispanic cops found in some of the smaller departments thought they were too good to apply this tactic. As for me, I often went out of the way to stop by and introduce myself as police officer who lived in the area. And although I did not directly work for the agency who had jurisdiction over their establishment, it gave them a sense of reassurance that someone with a badge had acknowledged their existence. I then headed for the house. After giving it some thought I decided to call some of the papers and share my story in hope that one of their reports would find interest.

My first contact was to a newspaper called "El Crucero." After a brief conversation with the reporter and a description of the facts it appeared at first as if he had serious interest in the story but that quickly died out as the week passed. It wasn't until after this incident that I took a closer look at some of the articles and topics that this paper had written about to discover that they were more concerned about issues in every corner of the world except Nashville. I looked page after page and could not find one of the many negative issues that impacted the Hispanic community on a daily basis, and in this area there were lots of them to choose from. I was astounded as to the fact that we were about to elect the first African American President and anti-Hispanic sentiments were at an all time high. It was disheartening to see that this Spanish language newspaper, like many others, chose to comment on everything to include a ran-over skunk in Brazil but none cared to comment on issues that affected the Latinos here in Nashville and in this part of the country. They hid from the issues at hand like a cheap Las Vegas Strip prostitute hiding from the Vice Squad. Several other Spanish language media sources met with the same results. This paper was a joke and served no purpose to the Hispanic community.

However, there was a small but fast growing Spanish paper that showed some interest. This Spanish paper was operating out of the Knoxville area and during one of his routine delivery runs to the Nashville area Carlos chose to go out of his way to stop by and collect all the details relating to the story. Two hundred miles out and running ahead of schedule Carlos called from just outside the city limits. I gave him directions to the house and within minutes he was pulling up to the driveway. I could see the expression on his face like most that visited expecting to find a rougher and somewhat rundown neighborhood. The Middle Class scene was a rarity for Hispanics in this region. He had the usual look most portrayed wondering if he was at the correct location. So I stepped out to meet him and after a traditional Spanish greeting along with a customary hand-shake I directed him to the living room where I had prepared everything I had. I could not wait to display the mountain of evidence I had long waited to share with any media source that showed interest. At first he appeared stunned and impressed and at the same time not knowing what to think or expect. If I had to guess what was going through his head it would be that he probably thought I was a cop hater with some psychiatric issues or an imposter with a badge. Or maybe a renegade cop who had gone over the edge. I showed him my credentials along with the many pictures from back in my military days which I had on display on the living room wall. Pictures don't lie and neither does statistical documented evidence. He appeared stunned and impressed like the many before him but after gaining his confidence I threw everything I had at him cherishing this golden opportunity of getting the word out and about. He asked about Puerto Rico and how recent immigration laws affected the people of the island. The answer was easy. "It doesn't." I said to him. He asked me to explain why so I pulled out a book with an old picture of American forces marching down the main dirt thoroughfare of a small Puerto Rican town and how the 16,000 troops encountered almost no resistance from the greatly out-numbered and out-gunned Spanish forces. The history lesson continued from July 25th of 1989 when the U.S.S. Gloucester steamed into Guanica Bay located on the southern coast where it endured seventeen days of hostilities to the Spanish-American War. I concluded the lesson with the signing of The Jones-Shafroth Act of 1917 granting citizenship to all citizens of Puerto Rico. Many Puerto Ricans believed that the Act allowed conscription to be extended to the island, which sent 20,000 soldiers to the US Army during World War One. In reality, however, the Act was under consideration long before the United States entered the War, and male residents of the United States, which at that time included Puerto Rico, were eligible for the draft whether or not they were U.S. citizens or nationals. I think I overwhelmed him with information and I was careful not to scare him off. I remember him asking me "Who is the lawyer representing you?" I said to him "No one, I am representing myself." He looked at me shocked and asked "You are representing yourself?" I looked at him and said

"Yes, I am representing myself." I was expecting for him to ask me a third time but instead he asked "How do you know so much about this?" My only answer to him was that I had spent some time around federal court. He did not waste any time pulling out his camera and tape record. He could not believe the dates on some of the letterheads with the original signatures. At one point he pointed at my very first piece of illustration as he said "This letter is dated 1993. You've had this piece of documentation since 1993?" My answer was "This one and a lot more." I pointed out the names of the commissioners who had been long gone and even the last one who was booted out thanks to the Kroll report and all the scandals of corruption that broke out a few years back. I could tell he was amazed as I reminded myself that the life of a lawyer is not to amaze but to prove a point to the court and get the job done. He jotted down every bit of detail he could get and stated it would be a front page story on the very next edition for certain and that it did. Later that month I found myself on the front page of Tennessee 's largest bilingual newspaper. The following edition ran a large block-character headline in both English and Spanish proclaiming:

HISPANIC FILES SUIT AGAINST THE STATE OF TENNESSEE FOR EMPLOYMENT DISCRIMINATION

Similar stories in this region were unheard of which met Carlos would have little competition and had asked for exclusives to the story. He did a superb job in his article. He wrote about the latest census report which showed that Hispanics grew 278% in Tennessee from 1990 through 2000. Evidence of such could be seen walking the streets of Chattanooga, Nashville, Shelbyville, and several other locations throughout the state and how the increase in the Hispanic population brought fear to local politicians of losing their long-held power and control. His article went on to say "Those coming from other countries, communities, and cultures sparked the fear of change." He further wrote "An American citizen who looks Hispanic and whose name sounds Hispanic, such a fear of foreigners is nearer to discrimination."

Wonderfully analyzed and perfectly written. And throughout the state many from the Anglo, African American, and the Latino communities read about a man alone on a mission. And many read about U.S. District Judge Aleta Trauger and her decision that claims against the state were strong enough to move this case forward to trial. He added "Mr. Laureano said after all is said and done, the Hispanic community will continue to grow and he would like to see a change in the way this agency handles the hiring of minorities."

A historical moment that would hardly be known along with the fall of the regime at highway patrol and the governor's response wrapped up the headlines by stating "The changes we make today are another step toward eliminating the decades old indolence of politics in the Highway Patrol and ensure that the leadership and management of the Department of Safety reflects the dedication and professionalism of the men and women in uniform who keep our highways safe and secure."

Alone on a mission to make a change, "I really like the way that sounds." I said to myself as I proudly posted a copy of the front page of that paper on the bulletin board by the church entrance. Two weeks later I found the paper tossed in a corner probably blown away by a strong breeze and on the bulletin board where the article once displayed was a for sale ad for a used car.

I eased off from any media sources after that day. I figured if the non-Spanish media wanted the story they would have to come and get it. Besides, I had more important things to worry about. The Pre-trial conference day was two months away. As for the defense, they were sitting ducks ready to be sunk.

Throughout the summer police work continued and every once in a while I would hear of cases of rouge cops, crooked lawyers, and low-paying government workers harassing area immigrants from many of my acquaintances, friends, and even fellow officers. From Berry Hill to the Town of Smyrna incidents arose that would blow my mind. I heard it all. Backed with the armor of ignorance and the areas quest to beat the nation in immigration enforcement made local cops assume they were the INS's faithful sidekick. With nothing in common but a government check these wanna-be ICE agents took racial profiling to an all new level. Jumping over each other to make a bust, the area bloomed with traffic stops as the days passed like a runaway epidemic without a cure. The endless number of illegal traffic stops went unchallenged to the degree that would save local police departments million of dollars in damages. A broken headlight would have an unexpected immigrant on a first class ticket south of the border. The new wave of immigration law enforcers and their quest to fix the flawed immigration system did more harm than good. The lack of knowledge of federal immigration laws did nothing but compete with the already ill-fated lack and ignorance of local laws. The rhetoric had everyone wearing a badge fighting for the top gun title of most arrests. Low paying government employees in various public service locations had the Feds up at arms. In the City of Clarksville a drivers license testing station employee became frustrated with a lady who had difficulty speaking the English language and confiscated her current driver's license accusing her of being an illegal alien and accusing her of a ridiculous crime. The lady was a U.S. citizen from Puerto Rico and was forced to miss her flight due to the fact that they confiscated her only form of identification. Rumor had it she was a relative of a Ft. Campbell soldier. The ineptitude of local law enforcement fueled with racial bias had the federal immigration agents dreading their every call. Federal agents came from as far as Memphis on bogus calls. The wasted valuable time and resources responding to senseless calls had INS agents cursing the locals all the way back to Memphis.

Several years back Mario had asked me to interpret for a client of his at the Nashville General Sessions Court. Delighted to help at no charge to anyone including the taxpayers I made my way into town that afternoon. Parking in downtown Nashville took a short time to find and as I walked into the courtroom I headed straight for the defendants table where I met up with Mario. The person on the stand was the Metro officer who conducted the traffic stop. Mario's brother who was assisting with the case started the questioning. The stop originated on the interstate where she claims to have been parked on the grass just off the shoulder. The questions continued in order to allow the court to get a picture of the chain of events. She claimed that the reason for the stop was what officers called the drive. Mario's brother asked her "What exactly is the drive?" She stated that it was when a driver would cling to the steering wheel so tight that you could see the white in his knuckles. She went on to say it included the driver looking straight ahead avoiding eye contact with the officer. After stopping the vehicle she obtained the driver's consent to search the vehicle. During the search she discovered a bag of illegal narcotics and all the occupants of the vehicle were placed under arrest for possession of a controlled substance. Then came the defendant. As I attempted to translate I began to get frustrated at the defendant's lack of common sense. The prosecutor sensed this and began to hammer at the defendant and began to parade him around like a clown. The defendant was being ridiculed and the court turned into a circus tent. It looked like a scene from Mayberry. I could clearly see the prosecutor was calling the bluff. I was forced to refrain from any involvement in the matter since I was entrusted in being completely neutral and truthful. As for my opinion, it did not count. When it was over and done with the court released the occupants due to the lack of probable cause and the driver was left with the charge. The experience was an unpleasant one as I struggle in a circle of chaos between an under-educated migrant worker, a smoke-blowing prosecutor, a fly-by-night cop, and a courtroom full of Nashville 's grade-A losers and villains laughing it up like a front row audience at comedy central. As we left the courtroom I looked over at Mario and said “Mario, correct me if I am wrong. Nowhere in that scenario did I see any probable cause for initiating a stop. In my few years in law enforcement I have never heard of the drive.” Mario replied saying “It appears to be a case of DWH.” I asked him “What is DWH?” And he replied “Driving While Hispanic.” I looked back at him and replied “Well, of course!”

Like fumes from the Yucca Mountain nuclear waste dump spilling over into its surroundings, DWH seems to have drifted south and into the town of Smyrna. If you were Hispanic and were caught driving without a driver's license on a second offense the small town judge in Smyrna would throw you in jail for thirty days. A narcotics trafficker had a better chance of obtaining leniency from the court. Like a cancer deep within the Nashville city limits is the notorious town of Berry Hill who arrested a pregnant Hispanic woman after conducting a warrantless stop. I was enlightened about this incident one night while sitting at the station checking my electronic mail. Local immigrant rights organizations would often forward updated information to me and this one was about a printed article that appeared on their website alleging:

IMMIGRANT MOTHER SUFFERS INHUMAN TREATMENT BY LAW ENFORCEMENT

The article went on to explain that on the 3rd of July a Berry Hill police sergeant pulled over the woman on the streets of this one-horse town. He never explained to her why she was being pulled over but the arrest warrant indicated careless driving. When I read this I looked over at my partner and said to him "The most famous made up charge a police can fabricate." The pregnant woman was forced to sit in a hot car for over an hour. At first she was told to call a family member who could drive her and her children home but when the police officer returned to her car he told her to kiss her kids goodbye and was immediately ordered into the patrol car or she would be hand cuffed. The first thing that came to my mind was that some racist desk sergeant or dispatcher sitting down at this rundown station house suggested he take her in and call immigration. She informed the officer that her baby was due in three days but this jerk with a badge could care less. As I read the article I looked at my partner and said to him "Doesn't this fool know the "cite and release" statue?" The more I read the worse it got. As every well trained cop knows the state general assembly has found that the issuance of a citation in lieu of an arrest of the suspect committing a misdemeanor crime will results in cost savings to the tax-paying public and frees up the jails for dangerous individuals or felons. This is what is known as cite and release. But knowing the ignorance that runs ramped throughout the many law enforcement agencies in this area it was clear to me that some wanna-be ICE agent back at the station suggested these actions. I looked over at my partner and said "How stupid can a person get?" He walked over and read part of the article and as he did I said to him "I am glad we don't work with guys like that at this department." No probable cause would tell any officer to stay clear. The only thing Berry Hill had going for them during this incident was that their low-budget cars lacked in-dash cameras. If they did this officer would get first prize on America's dumbest criminals. It wouldn't take a genius to figure out who the criminal would be on this clip. But it did not stop there. To add insult to injury the Davidson County Sheriff's officer continued the detention and while knowing of the pregnant woman's medical state they kept her in detention anyway. Three days later her water broke and she was transported to the local hospital. The sheriff's deputy assigned to guard the hospital room made it clear that a phone call to her husband was out of the question and the tattooed covered ape yanked the phone off the wall. This reject cop even denied her the use of a breast pump and she was told to forget about taking it with her back to the jail house. I worked with an officer that at one time had the misfortune of working at the Davidson County Jail and he informed me that half the time you could not tell the difference between the guards and the prisoners. He went on to say that most of the guards needed to be behind bars themselves. It was no surprise he left. Horror story after horror story and twenty five years too late, I finally understood what the Las Vegas Metro officer meant when he said the words:

TERRIFIED OF THE POLICE.

It was always easier to blame the immigrants then to look at the source. It reminded me of the day I walked into the driver's break room at my part-time gig and interrupted a heated conversation focused around illegal immigration. No one there knew about my day job as a cop so I helped myself to the conversation and innocently wandered off track from illegal activity in the form of immigration to illegal activity in the form of drug use. Thinking I was among a group dedicated to combating illegal doings I commented on my dissatisfaction with the company's weak frequency of drug testing. Hoping to get support from these fine citizens I observed as the room of concerned and law-biding fellow truckers slowly emptied out one by one to the point where I found myself standing alone. I asked myself "Did I say something wrong?"

Cops did some of the stupidest things. African Americans were no strangers to these types of injustices and although they remained quiet and rarely commented on these issues, they would never applaud these racist tactics and local leaders knew they could forget about counting on them for any support. News of this negligence faded in and out like a distant desert AM station and very few activists protested this behavior. Local Hispanic lawyers were making a killing ripping off the many low educated and naïve immigrants. I heard of cases where many immigrants and Hispanics paid thousands in legal fees to lawyers only to be left in court without representation and later returned to jail where they would sit for weeks to come. Month's worth of income gone with the wind.

There have been several occasions in the past where I found myself in an awkward position. I was in a room full of people along with another police officer or two when my good friend Pastor Rivas respectfully asked us about the unprofessional conduct of certain officers. The other officers justified the actions with irrelevant excuses. When it came my turn I told it like it was. The sentence usually started with "The law is quite clear. If there is no justification I don't do it." The response always brought the room to a stand still and as the topic of discrimination and racial profiling continued up for discussion the usual last words out of my mouth before leaving were, "They will have to fire me before I commit that crime. Besides, a desk job with a view at thirty five thousand feet I can easily get used to."

There was a time when a local Hispanic lawyer was asked to visit my pastor's Spanish congregation. She had an office in Nashville and identified herself as one who specialized in Immigration Law. One early evening she arrived at the church location and began taking questions and after answering the third question I knew she was full of hot air and her slow leak hissed the sound of a classic Las Vegas blackjack bluff. After forty five minutes of fooling the congregation she picked up her check from the pastor and headed out the door. Ninety-nine percenters never assume that somewhere in the crowd and usually sitting in the back might lurk a cop with the talent and skill of detecting a con-artist.

Hispanic celebrities had influence and pull but rarely became involved with such a cause. Any controversy could affect the status of their fame and hinder their pocket book which made this crowd undependable.

I was also invited to many gatherings among businessmen and other local area movers and shakers. I rarely turned down an invitation since it gave me an opportunity to show my face and being there automatically made my opinion count. I would not hesitate to respectfully voice my thoughts and although few did not care for my criticism towards their lack of progress and change for the better, I knew I paid cash for the ticket in and they weren't about to give me a refund. I was not too merciful with this group for the reason that very few represented non-profit organizations and establishments providing service to the minority community. Most all were there for a quick buck. I was very familiar with these cats and you always had to be on guard and they always had their hands in your pockets. This was also my least favorite crowd. The first question that came out of their mouths was the same every time. "So, what do you do for a living?" My answer was always the same. I identified myself as a police officer assigned to a federal facility who did some side work in the realm of construction and remodeling. I sometimes threw in my truck driving side gig. The arrogance floated through the air like a dead skunk. It was like everyone competed with each other to see who could impress the most. The only advantage of appearing at these "look-at-me" conventions were to make contacts with those who were in a position of decision making authority and could open the door to those I would send their way. There were some in the group I would meet who were honest and down to earth entrepreneurs. They were easy to spot and were usually the folks in the not-so-elegant attire, the semi-groomed hairstyle, and periodically broke a smile. The rest were the usual financial fakes that had a reputation to maintain. They kissed each others wallets and often showed their rude and shroud businessman demeanor. They did not intimidate me nor did they have me fooled. I had a purpose to serve and money meant nothing to me. I had to be careful at times. In this setting if you did not play your role in the act and did not wow to the status these folks portrayed you were sometimes construed as an unwanted guest whose jealousy fueled your anger. I walked away from several of these allegations just to avoid a confrontation but occasionally I would stand my ground and make clear to these folks that they were seriously mistaken. There was a time or two when I would respectfully informed them "The only people I am jealous of are those who are debt free, have not credit cards, and have a net worth so big that would make the bank sick to its stomach." But this was rare and most of these cats were too high on themselves, also referred by some as a legend in their own mind. This usually went in one of their ears and out the other and I was not going to let them reap the glory at my expense.

I spent most of the summer participating in the many bogus community meetings organized by rouge politicians benefiting from the soon approaching elections. Even some local broke businessmen and the all too many financial fakes appeared at these events. I often appeared unannounced and unknown to many if not all in these meetings. My strategy was to enter the room and cut right through the middle. Then I would head straight to the back where I would quietly sit and observe with a pen and a small notepad in my hand. I always encountered the same results. As I made my appearance and walked through the room there was almost always a drop in the volume that echoed from the mindless chatter in the place. Usually a few decibels. Some would stare and others would ignore. I was not much for the business attire except when in the courtroom or at an interview for an exceptionally well paying job and not just any jog. Everyone who knew me knew that when I put on a suit I met business and not the financial type either. But these groups of mislead fools and financial fakes weren't worth wrinkling the polyester. That stayed in the closet and out came the jeans and close knit shirts which was good enough for the mission. Besides, what you see is what you get.

That same summer a local wanna-be political figure was running for the position of State Representative. She had a fool-proof tactic for advertising her campaigned. All over Rutherford country were signs with her name posted at every intersection displaying "Stop Illegal Immigration." And in these parts you were guaranteed to get a hefty amount of support on that issue. Most of the support came from ignorant and racist butt-scratchers that considered every dark colored face an illegal immigrant. And she wasn't about to clarify that dilemma at the frisk of a drop in the poles. And it worked to her advantage and for other politicians in the area as well.

The local TV station one night aired a news report of an intoxicated assembly man thanking his group of supporters and at the same time venting his frustration at the fact that his competition was a republican Hispanic police officer. In his eyes the three lowest forms of society. From the looks of his gigantic protruding belly and his cheap suit, he was having as much trouble buttoning his blazer as he was standing up. It seemed that the closest this pathetic soul has ever been to a gymnasium was the Chinese buffet next door. I don't know who looked worse, the overweight and badly out of shape crowd of supporters that were there to cheer him on or him.

There was another occasion when a small neighboring town on the south side of Nashville even had the audacity to hold an emergency community meeting to discuss the problems that arose from the growing immigrant community which they claimed impeded the town and its precious tax payers. I thought about showing up to that one too. Local news sources in the area were quick to interview and obtain comments and opinions from the few Hispanic faces in the crowd. However, upon discovering that I wasn't and undocumented immigrant and even worse, a police officer, the reporters were quick to discard any on-the-air interview. This was also advantageous to the rouge politicians since it prevented them and their supporters from looking like a bunch of ignorant fools. If I decided to appear I would often get some type of the dirty look. I did notice that I was younger than the average guest. I did not know whether the looks were the result of having a dark skin tone or a well shaped physique.

Most departments had the advantage of providing a gym for their officers. A place where one could work to improve his physical fitness, turn fat into muscle, and strengthen his endurance. But what was most important to me and took priority over the rest was looking good in uniform. Having a fashion model's physique has never been a prerequisite in law enforcement and by the looks of the departments in this area one would guess that it would probably work against you as a disqualifying factor. And in most of these embarrassing and unethical cases, the sloppy appearance of the officer went hand in hand. As for the department providing the gym, it seemed like the only visitors were the roaches out for their midnight snack.

One day while on routine patrol I happened to be sitting in my patrol car surfing through the AM dial when I came upon one of Nashville's largest Spanish talk radio shows. The show was hosted by a man named Jose who was known by the Latino community as a no none-sense straight shooter. He had been hosting the show for several years and that day he had touched on a topic that got my attention. Crime was at a stand still and the two-way radio had been silent for almost an hour. The only type of activity at that moment was the aircrafts flying overhead on final approach to the local airport and the steady flow of afternoon traffic moving up and down Highway 231. So I reached over to the passenger's seat and I grabbed my cell phone and gave him a call to comment and voice my concerns and opinions about the issue at stack. And I told him just that. At first he could not believe what he was hearing and thought is was some type of joke. He said to himself "A cop criticizing the unethical actions of cops. That's something you don't see everyday." After realizing what he had on his hands he wrote down my contact information and invited me to the station's annual celebration as his special guest. We kept in touch throughout the months and that day I informed him of the latest out-come and this time he asked me to appear as a guest speaker on his up-coming show. That following Sunday I arrived at the radio station. I had a well prepared script in hand and was ready to go on the air. Jose did an excellent job with his no-holds-barred tactics of getting his point across. He started the show live at ten o'clock on the dot but to my surprise the other speaker that was also scheduled to appear ran into a scheduling conflict which caused her to cancel leaving the entire two hour slot to me. Ten minutes into the show Jose began asking questions in perfect chronological order. Inch by inch he gained closer to the point. He used this tactic in order to paint a perfect picture in the minds of his listening public. The signal covered far south across the state line into Northern Alabama and as far north as the City of Clarksville and over the state line into Kentucky. The microphone was mine and I let loose like machine gun fire. I was live on the air broadcasting the recent chain of events to all that heard. Every listener tuned in like a viewer glued to a television set. We told it like it was but something not quite that unusual happened that afternoon. We got about three calls none of which were directly related to the story. I think I knew why and found this understandable. It was a topic that had a certain level of importance to all that listened. However, many of those listening were also aware of the obstacles they faced with their current immigration status and that applying the same methods of seeking justice as the voice on the other side of radio would not work for them. But there was one particular place of interest receiving the signal loud and clear. Just north of the metro area was the small City of Clarksville which housed a moderate population of Hispanic inhabitants and just to the west of the city sits Ft. Campbell, a military installation which is home to one of the areas largest concentration of Hispanic soldiers. Most of those soldiers assigned to this post have ancestry from parts of central and South America and many are of Puerto Rican decent. Details of the entire case were soaked in by the many Hispanic soldiers and their dependants as well. The news of the Department of Safety's and the highway patrol's illegal hiring practices along with their closed-door tactic that resulted in years of discrimination towards Hispanic veterans fueled the outrage that most saw as a blatant slap in the face to the Hispanic veteran. But the outraged veterans chose not to comment and the Department of Safety and the highway patrol's disgraceful actions could not be commented or condoled by the post. The Department of Defense was quick to point out that they had nothing in common with the state but the land they shared. News of the broadcast discretely scattered throughout the area among Hispanics. To no surprise, Clarksville's only newspaper refused to print.

Not too far down the road I received calls from Latinos and even some from other minority groups asking me to help them file their cases. Flattered by the requests I had no choice but to inform them that the only thing I was good at was employment discrimination and civil rights. While on the air I made it clear that the message was not intended to scare or unmotivated but to prepare possible victims of similar crimes to be alert and not be caught off guard. Police officers are routinely taught that distinguishing a crime and knowing how to effectively react is always a plus. Whether on the streets, at the park, or in grocery stores I ran into friends and acquaintances who happened to catch my voice on the air. One even referred to me as the "Freakin Rican" a title I did not care to have. It was a good feeling to know that the message got out and was received by many. It made me realize that the time on the air was an effective means and time well spent. I also made clear that I was not there looking to gain celebrity status and that this was a one time event with hopes of making a change for the better.

Somewhere in the mist of this ocean of sharks I was relieved to have encountered some honorable and respectful groups largely devoted to civil rights. One particular group was the Tennessee

Immigrant Rights Refuge Coalition and from the first visit to their office I was astounded as to the efforts of this non-profit organization. Their dedication and effort stuck out above the rest and their respect and devotion to civil rights showed as clear as day. It became obvious that some standardization of influence was needed to avoid chaos. Financial gain was never in the picture and although you never heard much about this group it only convinced me more that today's society was and is clearly programmed with fear to avoid thinking outside the box. Because of the compulsive need for order and definition, organizations like these have developed a magnificent system for making a passage to meet their goals. And a fine job they did. Their effort to the cause was so strong and their message was often so loud that they got their message across every single time. I was impressed. The most overused warning that is told by most today is "Don't try to fight the system." To most that would seem reasonable until you look at the boundaries of the warnings which most never do. That is one area you will never find me. As far as I am concerned the sky is the limit. And that month I added them to my long list of organizations that have my financial support. It was money well spent for a good cause. Later that month I was invited to their Annual Celebration where I was treated as if I was an honored guest. The fact of the matter was that every guest that arrived that day was treated like an honored guest.

CHAPTER FIVE

A chance to make a change

One morning during a routine visit to my physician's office I found myself driving by the office of an acquaintance who I had met earlier that year with the help of some prominent area doctors. I happened to be in the area and elected to stop by and say hi. Goldy was the president of the Rutherford County Chapter of the NAACP and had been working for a successful mortgage company for a short period of time. That morning I arrived unannounced and was fortunate to catch him in his office. I greeted him and sat down in his office to update him on the status of my recent accomplishment relating to this exhausting but yet historic case. I happened to bring with me the most recent order and memorandum submitted by the court. He looked it over and reacted in the same manner as many before him. After reading the paragraph containing the words "will go forward to trial", he paused with amazement and shook my hand. As he congratulated my efforts he said " I don't know if anyone could have gone this far." Most people in your position would have given up. I thanked him for the compliment and shared with him my disbelief in the sense of not being able to find any form of legal representation interested in supporting my case. This comment was not surprising to Goldy as he expressed his feelings of knowing today's lack of interest in civil rights and the vast growing cases of employment discrimination. Goldy said some words to me that I will remember for the rest of my life. He looked at me and said "I have been fighting battles all my life." This comment was somewhat saddening but a reassurance of the fact there are still some willing to bare the burden of battle. The words came across like a true general with years of experience behind him. He also mentioned the name of an area lawyer given to him in the recent days and described him as one heavily involved and experienced in similar cases. His law firm was located in the City of Brentwood which was known as home to many country music celebrities, doctors, and even a few professional football faces. Brentwood was to Tennessee what Beverly Hills was to California. The name Brentwood alone was enough to get someone's attention and his firm was the largest in town. But it still didn't get my interest and I looked at Goldy and said "Goldy, I have been through them all and have seen them come and go." He responded in an understanding manner and said "It's worth a try." And from Goldy's desk we called his office and for a brief moment shared the details with the receptionist who asked us for a faxed copy of the last order. She ended the conversation by informing us that the copies were in her hands and that the attorney would look them over and that he would return my call shortly after. Thinking to myself that all this was just another waste of time I concluded the call and continued my visit with Goldy sharing stories of past events. The following day I got a surprising call from their office stating that the attorney had reviewed the latest order and was interested in talking with me in person. The appointment was set for the following day and early that morning I was off to the City of Brentwood. As I approached the office buildings in the area I was impressed. They displayed an array of the modern architecture. I entered through the main entrance and made my way up to the fourth floor. As I exited the elevator I was star-struck by the luxurious and elegant design of the lobby and the spectacular view of the city from its ten foot high semi-circular glass window. The layout was intriguing and every item was strategically situated to catch the attention and amazement of every passer-by. As I carefully made my way through this sculptured filled lobby and around the expensive artifacts I felt like I had just arrived at the Smithsonian Museum of Art. The office was one of two on this floor and as I approached the office entrance I could not help but to stop and admire the awesome view from the large lobby window. I presented myself to the receptionist and within seconds Larry came out to greet me. As we stepped into his plush office I could see the faxed copies of my order sitting on his desk. He sat down at his chair and picked up the copies holding them in his hands. He then informed me that he had reviewed them and came to the conclusion that it was a good case. This bit of information was certainly not new to me since it was something I had known from the start. He pointed out that the judge's decision to continue forward towards trial was a good sign. He also mentioned that the judge's strong scrutiny of Kerri's damaging affidavit would be highly beneficial to this case during trial. He said "I think we have a good case here." I said to myself in a manner not reflected towards him, "No kidding!" Now there was one thing left to discuss, the retainer fee. He threw an amount at me which I considered extremely reasonable compared to the few cowards I had spoken to in the past. I have had quotes as high as $10,000 from lawyers who had clearly demonstrated a serious lack of interest for my case. Most of which looked at me as if I was wearing a sign with the words SUCKER written all over it. With money in hand it was a done deal. I asked him "What about the up-coming pre-trial conference date?" He looked at me and said "I will take care of all that. All you have to do is sit there quietly and let me do all the talking." This was something I was not used to doing. I had baked the cake and it was not going be easy to stand there quietly while someone else put the icing on top. The important thing was that I had finally found a lawyer with the courage and the back-bone to fight for justice. I recalled many months back during a conference hearing set up by Judge Bryant. He had asked me if I had considered using the services of an attorney. My answer to him was "Your honor, I have tried looking for one but I don't see any lawyer taking on the state." He looked at me and said "There are some lawyers out there who aren't the least bit bashful about taking on the state." My only reply was "Yes your honor." I said to myself, "If there are they live in another state." The meeting lasted about five minutes and before I left his office he did need one other thing from me. He requested a list of names of anyone who I thought should be interviewed in a deposition. There were still a lot of questions to be asked and he was the man to ask them.

The first thing on Larry's agenda was to request and out-of-court settlement and to my surprise their response to him was made perfectly clear. They wanted trial and would not have it any other way. This arrogant "Bring it on" attitude was no surprise and in all reality came as music to my ears. Trial is exactly what I was hoping for. The following week I faxed Larry a list of everyone who I thought should be given the honor of sitting in the hot seat in a room for seven hours and virtually explain in perfect detail their involvement in this hiring practice that had impacted hundreds in the past. I had no problem coming up with such a list. And since this was something the defense would have never imagined would occur, it hit them by surprise. The list of names to be deposed was quite impressive. The list contained the names of the ex-commissioner who was ousted thanks to the findings of the Kroll report and the highest uniformed member of the highway patrol. Background investigators got front row tickets and we could not leave out the defense's star witness and her damaging affidavit. And the list went all the way down to the folks running the infamous recruiting office. The fax went out to Michael at the AG's office and within a matter of two days the "Bring it on" attitude swiftly turned into a "Can we talk about this?" mind set. When Larry filled me in on the details I asked him "What happened to bring it on?" He replied "When they received the list of names to be deposed they did a quick about face." Not surprising at all but I still wanted a trial. Right about that time the court ordered mediation which the defense had no problem agreeing to. It was also a desperate sign of relief for all of those on the list. Amazing how that works.

This month I took some time off and made a special trip to my all time favorite aesthetically minded destination, a trip to the place that I have always truly called home. I made it a point to revisit the island as often as I could. Out of all the places I have traveled, this was one exquisite place that topped all the others with its serene and tranquil setting. Every visit home I saw as a tropical playground that appealed to high end travelers and locals alike.

With over 300 miles of sun-drenched beaches that graced the famous coastline, Puerto Rico always made a timeless and idyllic setting for creating and reliving memories of a lifetime. It is no wonder that people keep coming back. And I was no exception.

On every visit I took a drive to an area located not too far from Old San Juan to my favorite spot along the shore. The route would take me past the old Naval Air Station which is now a shipping and container holding facility. And next to the shipyard is the original commercial passenger service airport which once served the island with World War Two era Lockheed Electras and Constellations. Today you might spot a few twin engine aircrafts and an occasional private jet. The local government had finally built a convention center which turned out to be one of the largest located outside the mainland. I had a favorite spot on the beach between two coconut trees where I would sit in the sand for hours at a time and enjoy the ocean breeze while watching the ocean-liners enter the port. The usual sight was that of passer-bys walking along the sandy beach or the ice cream salesman pushing his cooler full of treats. And not too far in the distant was the beachside bar and grill where guests would listen and dance to the rhythm of the island music while sipping on a pina colada with a touch of rum. And the only sound you would hear was that of the ocean waves and the neighborhood children playing on the beach. Not to mention the swaying of the palm tree leaves and a light tropical breeze. How could I complain, I was surrounded with world class dining, casinos, shopping, and a tropical rain forest only minutes away.

I looked at my watch and failed to realize that hours had passed. I felt the disappointing feeling of a great time coming to an end. So I gathered my belongings and started to walk back to my car before heading back to the inner part of the island. And as I walked I paused momentarily and took one last look back trying to convince myself of a good enough reason to stay a while longer. As I looked out towards the horizon where the sky meets the ocean I asked myself "Why would anyone want to leave this place?"

After a short lived two weeks, I was back on the plane trekking along over the skies of the Caribbean on a long journey back to the south for some unfinished business. As much as I wanted to remain on the island, I reminded myself that I had some unfinished business to take care of. They did not cut me a break and I was not about to cut them a break either. I may be a little late to the party, but definitely on track to a fashionable entrance.

June came around and the pre-trial conference kicked in and Larry made his appearance as counsel in court. And for the first time in years I entered the courtroom flashing the suit and headed straight for the plaintiff's table. I took off my blazer and placed it on the seatback of my chair. A behavior not practiced by many lawyers but not me. It was a sign of a relaxed posture and complete confidence. It is not the suit that makes the lawyer but his actions and his words. Larry noticed this and suggested that I keep it on throughout the conference. This hit me as a small reminder that I was no longer leading the convoying in this mission. But I took it as a bit of learning experience from a lawyer with years in the trade. And maybe somewhere behind this mysterious request was an infallible tactic which had served him well throughout the years so I complied and donned the blazer. I took my seat and sat there quietly for the entire duration. I did notice something out of the ordinary inside the courtroom. Sitting at the defendant's chair was a young man I had never seen before and there was no sign of Michael. At that moment Judge Trauger entered the courtroom and the bailiff asked the court to rise. As we got under way I learned that this mystery man was a substitute filling in for Michael who had an urgent situation to attend. As the conference started every question addressed to the defense resulted in the same manner. The response was always the same. "Your honor, I don't know." From day one the defense's courtroom performance and demeanors have been far from impressive. In all actually they have been down right wretched and embarrassing. At that moment I quietly thought to myself "Are those the only words that this defense team knows?" His third response was the same except that with this one he added "I am just filling in for the defense attorney assigned to the case." And that is about as far as we went. It was hopeless to try and get any progress from the mighty office of the Attorney General and their illustrious defense team so Judge Trauger continued by setting the trial date for August the 5th of 2008 and the court was dismissed for the day.

A few weeks transpired and the defense came to their senses realizing they did not have a leg to stand on. They pulled out of their suicide mission by agreeing to mediation which was set for September the 4th. When the date came around the suit came out of the closet and this one time fool for a lawyer headed for Brentwood for what was to become the final stages of this mission for change. But the events that occurred that day were so mind-boggling that to this day I still can't comprehend. It's a question that hovers constantly circling in my head day after day.

I appeared at Larry's office as expected ready to face my long time opponent while keeping a watchful eye out for the element of surprise. Before entering the conference room we talked about what was expected. I was somewhat relieved that this fourteen year journey was coming to a close. Larry informed me that all the work I had done impressed everyone in his law firm. He further stated that I had saved an enormous amount of money in legal fees by doing my own case. He also told me that any lawyer would have easily charged me approximately $80,000 in legal services. I said to myself "$80,000 for this? What an over-priced racket." I took it as another compliment to add to the list. After our pre-conference briefing it was show time. We stepped into the firm's elegantly designed executive style room. As I entered the room I saw Michael and like an old friend I felt this overwhelming urge to greet him. I noticed he was accompanied by another stranger I had never seen before. As I sat in the room I wondered the role of this unknown character and his purpose in this matter. I sat wondering about the many possibilities and went as far assuming him to be the State Attorney General, but never did find out. As the puzzling chain of events continued I sensed a certain mist in the air that gave me an uneasy feeling as I sat there quietly watching the actions of this mission for change come to light. The mediator assigned to the case was a man named George and from the minute he sprung into action I read him like a player at a blackjack table counting cards. Like a crop-duster spraying the landscape with a toxic nerve gas, the only thing greater than this enemy fighter's desire to kill this case was his huge price tag. As the gun fire began I could hear the words "run for cover!" And that I did. I sat there helplessly watching the spray of gun fire light up the sky like a fireworks display at Disneyland. Offers came and offers went. The one thing I was certain that would bring this battle zone to a halt was to call in an enemy strike. The boys in the air never miss. But calling out a request was futile as reality kicked in and I realized that I was no longer calling the shots. And as the gun fire slowed to a crawl this one time fool for a lawyer sat in the back seat watching this mission go to hell in a hand basket. When the gun fire stopped and the smoke cleared all that was left was the burning rubble of years of training, melding, and the finest armor blown to pieces. Stacks of ammunition never touched. The gruesome task of a casualty report.

All that remains is the anticipated question that comes from above.

MISSION ACCOMPLISHED?

CHAPTER SIX

When it's all said and done

What followed was a period of silence. A very unusual silence. There was no media coverage, no cameras or reporters trailing me for facts or details. No Hollywood style conspiracies. I reported to work as usual. No plot to bar my employment as a government employee at any government level. It was actually too quiet. It is almost like it never happened. Some say that what the public doesn't know won't hurt them. And maybe there is some true to that.

In the infamous place chosen to bare the name Sin City there is a well-known proverbial expression. The house always wins. In other words the house never looses. There is an exception to this glamorized myth and a fundamental certainty that is kept quietly hidden underneath the glitz and glamour. A well kept secret very few talk about. The thought alone is enough to make even this bold town tremble with fear. As long as there is the slightest possibility of a jackpot the city is sure to survive. Many years of trial and error have proven this to be true. Even rumors of a flaw in the system or a method designed to cut against the reality of a jackpot were not enough to implement the least bit concern to this town, and it can rest assure knowing that the fool and his money are sure to revisit. But even Las Vegas is well aware that when word hits the streets of an improbable chance of success, the town is guaranteed to flounder. My saying is if you don't play the game you won't loose either. And without any players the house will crumble. And around this place a player with a fool proof system of beating the olds is considered a symbol. A very dangerous symbol at that. Not too different from a Pro Se litigate beating the house in the world of litigation. Whether you're rocking the house in Las Vegas or rocking the house in Nashville, it's all the same thing. A dangerous symbol it is if it holds the ability of shaking loose the perfectly structured foundation of a billion dollar industry.

As for the make shift tent that provided shade for a rage-tag gang of political thugs. Well, it came dangerously close to crashing down and exposing a perfectly orchestrated hiring system strategically designed to facilitate them at the expense of Affirmative Action. It was a near miss for the Department of Safety. A trial canceled and a national embarrassment erased from the public eye. No media coverage, no deposition, no trial. They managed to dodge a class action lawsuit that would have had the state knocking at the door of bankruptcy court. It was pennies on the dollar. You can say things turned out quite well for them. Rumors came and rumors went. I heard it all. Everything from pay-offs to corruptive cohesion, sell-outs, and even allegations of plain cowardness. I never did find out who the mystery man in the room was.

As for the Tennessee Highway Patrol. Well, nothing really has changed. All seems well at Headquarters. The cars will roll towards their designated areas after row call and the helicopters will launch and fly their routine missions. As for the thugs at the administrative level, every once in a while the heat gets turned on and the Governor flushes them out only to replace them with a similar regime. It's just another day in this wild game of politics.

I recently heard that the Puerto Rico Legal Defense and Education Fund had changed its name to Latino-Justice. Gallivanting like a freshly recruited Sunset Boulevard call girl out browsing the shops of Rodeo Drive, new attire for this wolf in sheep's clothing does little to hide their true intentions. They still collect monetary contributions from the soldiers and sailors of the armed forces, the poor and low-income, and the innocent and naive. Behind the solid oak doors and their plush and luxurious office style setting the appearance is quite contrary to the low budget web-site and their cheap suits. The answering machine might kick in at the Media Relations office if it is not out-of-service. And if you are looking for information don't hold your breath. It's safe to assume they have no comment.

The Tennessee Human Rights Commission will always be around like a cancer without a cure. As long as the state can justify their need for existence you can be sure to see them like a caravan of clowns bringing up the rear of a parade.

Judge Trauger and Judge Bryant remain two of the finest people sitting on the throne at the Federal Court house. A symbol of hope fueled by compassion and armed with the awesome power of the world's greatest judicial system.

As for Michael, I never knew what became of him. My only guess is that he can still be found at the AG's office. I have no hard feelings towards him and I may have even been a little harsh at times. It is now that I realize that he was only doing what he was told to do. And a fine lawyer his is. I am sure he would make a very good State Attorney General.

The months went by and summer turned to winter. I rushed to wrap up all the outdoor projects around the house. As I cut the grass and painted the porch neighbors and friends would pause for a moment as they walked down the street to congratulate me on the so-called Million Dollar settlement. A simple thank you and a friendly waive was my way of responding but the guilt shot through me like cold water. "If they only knew," I thought to myself. I even got an electronic e-mail message from my old friend Juan who congratulated me as his guard unit prepared for deployment to the Middle East. Like thousands of others from all corners of the nation, all ages and races. I recalled how he stood by me all those years to listen to my tales of sorrow and who reacted silently not knowing what words to say or even wondering if words of encouragement would surpass the regret. It took all I had to hold back so I hesitated in responding knowing that the measly settlement amount could not buy a used subcompact in a rundown Volkswagen dealer. So I simply wished him the best of luck and a safe return soon. Whether it's a million or a hundred it really does not matter. Besides, I never saw a dime. One October afternoon I found myself making a trip to downtown Nashville to meet Mario for lunch. A chilly fall afternoon made for a pleasant stroll through the busy streets of downtown Nashville. The fastest route to downtown was via the interstate but that day I decided to take the old road. A twenty minute drive right to the heart of Nashville would take me by the airport. A road I had traveled many times over in the last fifteen years. The route would take me right under the final approach path of runway 20 Right. As I approached Donaldson Pike I could see an airliner on short final making a smooth approach right on the glide slope. I followed it all the way to the ground as he set the main gear on the threshold. They get it right every time. And off to the south side of Murfreesboro Road was an all too familiar sight. I have seen it a million times before and not much has changed in fifteen years. Right behind the old and semi-ragged tan colored highway patrol station appeared the taxiway lights, the all-metal hangers, and the orange colored wind sock. It's all the same and only the names have changed to protect the innocent. As I sat at the red light I took a closer look and I could see the hanger doors standing wide open. Not far within sat the elegant sight of the latest version of the Bell Jetranger helicopter shining like as if it just came off the assembly line. Mesmerized by its awesome sight, I neglected to notice the light turn green. A friendly tap of the horn from the car behind me reminded me of my lunch appointment. As traffic started to move and the car ahead of me pulled further away I could see a bumper sticker planted on the rear of the vehicle clearly displaying the famous words of the presidential hopefully-CHANGE. Not far from the airport was Mario's office on the 34th floor of the Renaissance Tower with a spectacular view that only an aviator would recognize. Every visit to his office made me admire the awesome view. "I could stand here for hours." I would say to myself. We made our way through the hustle and bustle of the streets of Nashville to a small Greek café off 2nd avenue where we reminiscent the last fifteen years of the hard work, long hours, and the dedication invested in our efforts for a better community and our contribution to civil rights. We compared the challenges from two different angles, two different lifestyles, and the same road. I got a glimpse of the court system from an Attorney's point of view as he shared a few educating words. He informed me that the court system's common practice of maintaining lengthy periods of delay was designed to discourage and dismiss cases. Little did he know that I had known that for many years. So I respectfully agreed and enjoyed the rest of his company. If any one deserves the title of attorney it was him.

One the way back to the house I drove past the Federal Court Building and something came over me. The feeling I got was that of the sight of an old house that I once lived in or a friend that I had not seen in a very long time. With hours to spare I pulled into the public parking area and headed straight to the main entrance. As I approached the front of the building I glanced up at this ten story symbol of justice. I walked passed the barricades and the night deposit box I became so acquainted with. The small army of security officers whose faces I was forced to remember. The visitor's log book was right where I left it and after signing in the elevator doors beside it came open. I stood to the side waiting for its passengers to disembark but no one was in it and no one stepped out. Like an old friend welcoming me, I boarded the elevator expecting to find the 8th floor bottom already lit. It was as if I was just there the day before. The launch of the elevator and its usual nauseous result lead me on a quick ride to eighth floor. As I walked towards the Court Clerk's office I came up on courtroom 775. There it was empty as always. I peeked through the twelve inch window and could see its floor highly polished and the furnishings shined like a new penny. I looked up at its gigantic ceiling. I could not help but to open the door and step inside and just for a minute I admired the elegant room where I sat and made history. I continued down the hallway past the clerk's office and went to the PACER computer system where I helped myself to the electronic files. And there I sat glancing at the last and final filing in my venture to justice. Curiosity kept hounding me and in order to please it I gave in. I thought about getting up and walking away. I looked at the keyboard and hesitated as I began punching in the case number. They say curiosity killed the cat but that day it killed more than just the cat. The last few motions filed were short and sweet. With little ink wasted and to the point. Electronically filed and no postage wasted. Technology may have done justice for the delivery boy but did little for the victim. As I read the last few motions of my case I came up on the one that hit me in the chest like the 9 AM express train. One that made me wish I would have kept on driving. Like a stab in the heart or a soldier disgraced with duty of informing his command of a mission incomplete. The words of a quitter in black and white, printed in large text and clear as day

MOTION TO DISMISS WITH PREJUDICE

on behalf of the plaintiff. The one that followed had the judge's seal of approval

MOTION GRANTED. Case closed.

Two months later history was made but not by me. But instead by the man who flew around the country in a plane with large three foot letters displayed on the side of his bird. The word CHANGE in large three foot letters that could be seen from the ground at five thousand feet. The nation had elected its first African American President. It was a symbol of hope and a symbol of change. And as this great nation of opportunity celebrated I could see hundreds of bumper stickers up and down the road and signs all over town displaying the word CHANGE. African Americans, along with the millions of Hispanics, celebrated this victorious moment of truth as they showed reverence to the man that would make that change. Everyone celebrated until the late hours of the night. The festivities began and everyone danced. From the rich to the poor, all ages and races. There were sons of immigrants and sons of slaves. There was no ticket to ride and all were welcome. Convicts and cops, soldiers and lawyers, truckers and pilots, they were all there. Money meant little at this spectacle and every soul standing was an honored guest. The door was wide open but this time I stood outside looking in through the large glass window struggling to see through the smoke and mist. As I watched this masquerade unfold my eyes glanced from one side of the room to the other in amazement. "Hispanics not welcomed?" Not at this masquerade. The disarrayed figures came in and out of focus and a small break in the crowd revealed a small familiar assemblage. And back in the smoke filled corner as they raised their glasses to render a toast I could see the faces of all of those who left me hanging out to dry in a battlefield that would make Normandy Beach look like the poolside lounge at the Cesar's Palace.

As for me, I heard about a small commuter operation that runs between Vegas and a couple of airports along the Southern California coast. It's been about seventeen years since I last flew at the controls over Southern Cal. The last time I flew anywhere near the southwest was in April of 99 when I wondered off on a long joy ride along historic route 66. I had read about it in a flying magazine and since I had driven the route many times I promised myself that one day I would fly that same route, and I did. I stayed low for the beginning of the trip and at twenty five hundred feet I got a bird's eye view of the country side. I stayed there until I reached the Texas panhandle. The change in the scenery was spectacular and the terrain was rising so fast that I was forced to seek a higher altitude. But I remained within a thousand or so above the ground in order to get the best view out of the trip. I had just topped the tanks in Tucumcari and was airborne again in under twenty minutes and headed westbound. As I came upon an intersection known to the locals as Cline's Corner I looked down just forward of the left wing and observed what appeared to be a tractor-trailer pulling a set of doubles with the rear trailer on its side and in the right travel portion of the westbound lanes. Out of curiosity I began to orbit the accident scene and did so for about five minutes with no sight of any emergency vehicles. I knew that there was nothing I could do from above so I stayed in the turn and as I approached a westbound heading I leveled the wings and started for the horizon. And as I did I realized that there was one thing that I could do. I recalled that there weren't many cell phone towers along that portion of the interstate in those days meaning that there was a good possibility that the authorities had not been notified of the accident. I also realized that at that moment I was what law enforcement agencies referred to as air support. You may have heard some refer to these talented aviators as the watchful eye in the sky. And for the first time in my life I found myself carrying out the role that America's finest has depended on since the first aircraft took flight. Without hesitation I made a hard bank left and returned to my circular pattern over the target. I pulled out my sectional map and was fortunate to have found a remote communications outlet approximately five miles west of Cline's Corner which was well within radio range. I tuned in to the frequency and called Albuquerque Flight Watch and asked the flight service specialist to telephone the New Mexico State Police and informed them of the accident. The flight service specialist was very helpful and stated that he would gladly make the call. I orbited for a few more minutes wanting to stay on the scene until the emergency vehicles arrived but fuel was precious and airfields in this region were few and far between. Most were abandoned desert strips that provided no fuel service. So I had no option but to break loose and continue about my merry way. One good deed done for the day and the end of a short lived life-long dream. I sensed a feeling of gratitude as I carried on with what was turning out to be a magic carpet ride out west. It was also another reminder that the finest things in life are free, and that everything else comes with a price tag.

I spent that evening at the Albuquerque International Sunport where I treated myself to dinner at a delightful Mexican Restaurant located at the passenger terminal across the airfield before heading back to the fixed base operator where I spent the remainder of the night resting at the pilot's lounge. The following day I was up early and in the air before sunrise trying to take advantage of the dense air. A quick fuel stop in Flagstaff met with an interesting departure. My low horsepower engine barely generated enough thrust to get me off the runway and the climb out was rough, but once out of the hole it was business as usual. I caught a peek of the west rim of the canyon and flew right over Hoover Dam like I had done many times in years past. As I flew over Hoover Dam it brought back memories of my early aviation years. The view over the valley was as spectacular as always and the only change was less desert and more urban sprawl. With the end of the rainbow in sight, it was just a matter of minutes and I would be on the ground.

My most recent journey was not all that much different then the one from ninety nine. It had been fourteen long years and it seemed like I had been to hell and back. As I made my descent into the Las Vegas Valley I looked outside the window and from nine thousand feet it all looked the same. The approach controller asked me if I was familiar with the Las Vegas area and although it had been quite some time since I had traversed the airways of this area I responded by saying "yes." I was directed to fly over the Las Vegas Wash and direct to downtown which would put me several miles from the traffic pattern at North Las Vegas. As I continued the descent I began to get a bigger picture of the many changes below. As the main gear touched down I felt a mysterious feeling come over me, one that I could not quite explain. It was as if for a split second time had stood still. Like a sailor reaching port to a foreign place, I approached the terminal building to conclude the first leg of what turned out to be a life-long ambition. A challenging but at the same time exhilarating cross country journey that most general aviation pilots would gladly trade for a coach ticket on a discount airliner with a fresh batch of peanuts, soft drinks, and a short in-flight movie. As I opened the door to the cockpit, the cool air that I had brought down with me from several thousand feet above the surface had quickly whooshed out the door and was swiftly replaced with the 104 degree heat wave that hit me in the face welcoming me to the place I once called home and the airfield I had spent long days and pleasant nights during my flight training days several years prior. I made it a point to spend a short amount of time out in the scorching temperature as I reminiscent the many days I was forced to tolerate the heat, sweat, and blowing desert dust out on the ramp as I conducted pre-flight and ground related procedures. I recalled the many hours spent parading in the fierce and unpleasant arid atmosphere and while most enjoyed the comfort of their air conditioned vehicles, I withstood the environment that would often put many dangerously close to heat stroke. I often wondered to myself if it was the result of the many years I endured in the tropics during my childhood days or being blessed with a gift from up above that empowered me with the health and physical strength to resist such harsh conditions. I even wondered if it was simply the reward of good Army training that conditioned me to ignore and resist the environment and allowed me to keep charging forward. Either way, air conditioning was not a luxury available in the small fleet of aging aircrafts available at the time. And if you wanted a pleasant flying atmosphere a short trip up to 9,000 feet would get you a modest 85 degree reading. It was better than nothing.

So I topped the tanks for the short leg that followed and chained the aircraft down for the night. I noticed the city had finally built an elegant Adobe style terminal building that gave private pilots an executive style welcoming. As I approached the door to the terminal I took a look up and could see the observation deck and patio of the terminal restaurant along with the few guests and aviation enthusiasts enjoying their outdoor meals as they watched over me like a celebrity who had just stepped off of a private jet. I stopped at the fuel desk and checked in with the attendant to pay for the fuel. I then made my way through the elegantly designed lobby and out to the passenger pick up area. My brother picked me up at the airport that afternoon as was the usual routine and we began to cruise the boulevards of what appeared to be a city in the midst of immense change. I observed my surroundings, looking through the passenger's window of the large pick up truck as we drove through an endless number of intersections. I was astounded as to the changes that blossomed as urban sprawl led the way for this oasis and it showed as we traveled the streets of North Las Vegas. Growth was evident and along with its many attributes, cultural diversity was the dominating scene as we drove street by street, intersection by intersection. Asian shopping centers as far as the eye could see and Mexican, Central, and South American businesses boasted the west coast influence. And not to my surprise, as I have said many times in the past, quietly nested in every corner of town one could still find traces of the charm and rich heritage of the Latino people. Still contributing to society like any other place, evidence of Hispanic families shedding their traditions and pristine culture was the view from this side of the window. It had never left, it just grew with its surroundings.

As the journey continued down Craig Road I observed as acres of desert that once enclosed the North Las Vegas Airport from my flight training days years back were taken over by industrial parks and office complexes. Business jets lined up in perfect unison on the opposite side of the airport's rigid security fence. The Craig Road jump zone where weekend parachuters once landed is now someone's back yard and the vast selection of vacant land that at one time comforted an unscheduled emergency landing would now have you up against the drive-thru window of one of the many local fast food franchises. Traffic resembled that of Southern California and the atmospheric setting made for an excellent day out on the lake.

We made an unscheduled stop at a trucking firm that was coincidently situated in an office complex just north of the airfield. As we approached the building we pulled up to the parking area located across from the main entrance and a shot of reality quickly changed the scene from what set out to be a pleasant welcome. The sight of careless employees loitering around the main entrance smoking and joking made for an unprofessional setting. I looked to my left as a member of the crowd approached the driver's side of the vehicle reminding me of the typical scene at a downtown drug point. My brother lowered the driver's side window and began conversing with what turned out to be mindless chatter. I tried my best not to eavesdrop on the conversation and only acknowledged my name as my brother introduced me to this stranger. A slight nod of the head and a week hello is all I received from her. I began to extend my hand out to render the traditional Spanish hand shake but quickly canceled this set of actions as I read the dry and anti-social expression on her face. The vibes were coming across loud and clear and it was all coming back to me like a dark distant memory from long ago. It was then that I realized that I was back in Sin City. So I saved her the burden of touching the hand of a dirty Hispanic and focused my attention on the derelict crowd outside the window. I quietly sat in the passenger's seat thinking about Nevada State Law covering designated employee smoking areas. The sight of a rather tall and slightly malnourished female with a cigarette in her mouth and a dangling left arm displaying needle tracks as clear as a Las Vegas billboard reminded me of the few skanky drug rehab patients on parole I had interacted with many times in the past. Her faithful sidekick, who chose not to participate in the smoking session, was three miles short of six pack abs and a nose pointed so far up in the air that it topped the peak of the Stratosphere Tower. I kept reminding myself that I was back in Sin City where greed, arrogance, and false smiles ruled with a passion. So I wondered to myself if it was a good time to test the waters. I answered to myself "Why not."

I opened the passenger's door of the rather huge pick up and stepped down while planning my strategy. I stood along side the truck looking for the main entrance and could feel that all eyes were on me like an undercover vice cop in the midst of a drug point. I proceeded towards the building playing the role of a costumer in need of assistance as every eye in this faction of losers tracked my every move. As I walked past the female spectator I inconspicuously glanced over at her left arm to confirm my suspicion but was distracted when I realized that the main lobby entrance was two doors down. I turned back in the opposite direction and swiftly made my way back through the zone of fire which I had just traveled. As I exited the gauntlet the test results were complete and precise. There was no greeting, no helpful directions, not even an offer of a cigarette. It appeared that this

Vegas showgirl candidate was more concerned about taking another puff of the cigarette in her mouth than customer service with a smile. A helpful hand would have been enough. But not this crowd.

I recalled being told sometime back that this outfit was a family operation which would explain the substandard service. This crowd of Vegas high society wanna-to-be's took lack of customer service to an all new level. They leased everything except a touch of class and a guidebook to a halfway decent physique. I then thought to myself "Welcome back to Las Vegas." I stepped inside the lobby of this reject trucking firm and paused for a second, I turned around and walk back outside making one last attempt in hopes of discovering some type of change for the better. I stood outside looking out into the horizon admiring where the vast desert valley meets the clear blue sky, all along trying to be inconspicuous of my true intentions. I glanced to my left and looked back in the direction of my brother's truck and the sorry crowd he associated with only to confirm that the appearance of a lost client meant very little to this gang. I observed as this crowd of losers in disguised looked over me like vultures hovering over desert prey. With every eye on me, I thought to myself while shaking my head "Welcome back to Las Vegas." Having nothing more to prove, I turned around and stepped back inside to the comfort of the air conditioned lobby and I said to myself "Some things will never change."

Then from a sort distance away I heard the sweet sound of ebony ask "Can I help?" I turned around as to see where the sound was coming from. At first I could not distinguish where the voice was coming from but as I took a closer look I saw from over the lobby counter, and partially hidden behind the rather tall standing receptionist station, was the sight of a lovely African-American woman, sitting there like a Memphis rose on the east banks of the Mississippi River. I was stunned as to the fact that someone had actually acknowledged my existence. I said to myself "Maybe there is still some hope." I looked at her momentarily noticing how she resembled a young African American woman who I was romantically involved with from back in my military days. Leave it to an African American woman to set the example. How ironic.

I told her that I was waiting on someone and made myself comfortable in the plush lobby sofa. I spent the next few minutes thinking about how some things just don't transmit neatly in black and white, but rather in many shades of gray. Somehow, and for some mysterious reason, a touch of the south must have drifted this way against the might Santa Ana winds and gently settled in this ruthless desert. Scientific studies have proven that with just the right setting even a rose can survive in the harsh and brutal desert.

It is safe to assume that not all things come to an end and some things do not ever change. Everyone who knows me knows money means nothing to me and that the finest things in life are free, and everything else comes with a price tag.

So I made the best of the few days left in this mystifying place. Every morning met with a routine cup of coffee at my favorite place. To my luck, there was a Starbuck's coffee franchise in virtually every hotel and casino on the Strip and in every corner of town. I took an occasional drive out to the desert to see Redrock Canyon and made it a point to visit the casino snack bar where I once cleaned tables and served popcorn many years ago. The original "Slots-A-Fun" sign still attracts the usual crowd and I could not resist trying one of the many foot long hot dogs and shrimp cocktails I had once prepared many moons ago. Twenty years later, and to my surprise, they were still on sale for ninety nine cents. Maybe some things are best left unchanged.

My mission there had come to an end and on the last morning I headed back to the airfield for the final leg of the journey. As I climbed up on the left wing of the aircraft I looked up at the sky and said to myself "Another fine day to be flying." This place had a reputation for having some of the best flying weather in the nation. Within minutes I was cleared for take-off and as I departed to the southwest I took one last look out the window to admire the bird's eye view of the valley from above.

But nothing beats the route between the Las Vegas Valley and Southern Cal. From what I can remember the route is awesome. At about three thousand feet you could see Lake Mead just off to the east of the Las Vegas Valley and the short flight over the Mojave Desert is a breath-taking sight. As you approach the El Cajon Pass you start to see the drastic change in the landscape. From dry desert to mountains and once you cross over into the south side of the San Gabriel Mountains it hits you in the face. Wall to wall suburbs, all the way to the coast. The twin engine high wing aircrafts operated by most commercial pilots in the area gives you an unobstructed view of the land. The more I think about it the better it sounds. It is certainly something to consider.

During my most recent visit to Southern California I had a chance to spend some time with another Army Comrade who now lives in the suburb of Santa Fe Springs. It is always good to see the guys after all these years and since I was in town I decided to call Eric and tell him that I was spending a few nights in a motel just off of the I-5 not far from Disney. He drove down and met up with me in the charming poolside patio area the motel had provided for its guests. We chatted all night and covered a few topics such as life in Southern California, law enforcement, and a few other things. He said to me "You know that just about every good size department and every sheriff's office in this area has an aviation unit and they are always looking for a few good pilots. But there is one catch." I asked "What's that?" He added "You have to start as a patrolman and make your way up through the ranks." I looked at him with a motionless look on my face as I said "You don't say?" I skipped out on the coffee that night and instead we walked across Ball Road to the gas station across the way and purchased a good old fashion California fruit drink. The streets were busy that night and there was a lot of tourist activity out and about. With a light ocean breeze and the temperature at a pleasant seventy five degrees it made for a typical California evening. We jolted across traffic to the other side and back to the patio to finish the drinks. All good things come to an end and it was late in the night. Interstate traffic had lighten and Eric had to get back home and as he walked to his car he looked at me and said "If you're interested in staying in police work you know Spanish speaking officers are always in demand." I hollered back at him "What makes you think that?" And as he closed the door he stuck his head out of the driver's window and hollered "We're in Southern California!" As I waved him off I said "Right." And as I headed back to the motel room I noticed a large poster that the motel owner had displayed behind the glass window of the main lobby. I stopped to examine the photographer's fine sense of artistry. He timed it just right when he took the picture of the sun setting over the horizon out in the pacific. I can tell the awesome sight of that sunset anywhere. It looked just like I saw it from my childhood years living in Los Angeles. And printed on the very top of the poster I saw the words California Sunset. I stood there admiring the photographer's expression of this majestic place and for a split second I thought to myself "California , I could get used to this place."

Carlos nailed it right on target when he wrote "When it's all said and done."

THE END

For now, but I'll be back

Made in the USA
Monee, IL
04 November 2026

67388647R10066